Network Marketing For Facebook

The Workbook

Jim Lupkin, Marianne Lupkin & Brian Carter

"Why a Network Marketing for Facebook Workbook?
Because we need to stop just reading, and start *doing.*
I like step-by-step actions steps. Action is what will get us results.
So using proven techniques that work on Facebook to build
real relationships is our number one strategy. And that is how to
make Facebook a key part of your business building portfolio.
So don't just read this workbook. *Use it!*"

- Tom 'Big Al' Schreiter

DEDICATION

Every now and then, men come along who
change the course of history. Mark Yarnell was one of those men
for the network marketing profession.

People call him a legend. We call him a friend. Through the power of
network marketing, combined with his gentle and compassionate spirit,
Mark touched the souls of millions. He saw greatness in everyone.

Jim says, "I consider Mark Yarnell to be my only teacher in network
marketing. Everyone else is a colleague."

At 24 years old, Mark took Jim under his wings and taught him how to
be a network marketing professional. Mark and Jim worked closely
together, even having phone conversations at 2 a.m. Mark's teachings,
along with Jim's passion for social media, laid the foundation for the
Network Marketing for Facebook series.

The network marketing community suffered a great loss when Mark
passed away in 2015. Though he is no longer with us, he lives on
through our teachings. We hope we can take the torch and continue to
spread Mark's light.

This workbook is dedicated to Mark Yarnell.

Network Marketing For Facebook Success Stories

50 new distributors in 2 weeks thanks to Network Marketing For Facebook!

"You have helped so many people add value to their business because of your knowledge and hard work in the field. Just over a two week time frame we added 50 new distributors to our team thanks to Network Marketing for Facebook. A few of our team members got together and decided to focus on specific types of people every two weeks. We took advice from your book by changing our cover photos to align with our mission. We reached out to prospects who showed interest and invited them to our team page to create more exposures so they could read success stories from other team members. We focus on recognition and attracting others based on our daily lives. When it comes to exposing others we simply recognize someone's results on our program."

– Brad and Sonya Wildermuth

$2,162.05 in commissions and 4 new distributors in 37 days thanks to Network Marketing For Facebook!

"I have had 2.5 years in my current network marketing business and yielded little results until I started to follow Network Marketing For Facebook – specifically graph search, establishing a post balance and sharing more on FB about my products. Before reading this book, I would go 6-8 months with no notable commissions. I gave myself the test period of February 21st – April 30th and in that time my commissions (between my company, Paypal & Square transactions) equaled $2,162.05 and I have added 4 new distributors. I am PUMPED!!!"

– Tamara Davis-Jack

More than 6 new customers and 2 new consultants thanks to Network Marketing For Facebook!

"I've never had more people approach me about the product and opportunity since I've changed my way of Facebook marketing. I would like to thank Jim Lupkin and Brian Carter for writing Network Marketing for Facebook. After reading, I was able to recognize everything I was doing wrong, and have learned how to do it right. Whether you are a novice or professional 'Facebooker,' each chapter is written in easy-to-read language, guiding you step by step. Between my team and I, we have connected with old friends, made new friends, sent out more samples, gained more than 6 new customers and 2 consultants. I continue to read the book daily so my success continues! This was within 3 weeks of reading and following the book."

— Heidi Riddles

66% increase in business, 50 orders and 2 new distributors thanks to Network Marketing For Facebook!

"I picked up the Network Marketing for Facebook Book at the suggestion of a friend. I was amazed at the simple system in this book that was so incredibly easy to apply to my business. I immediately read the book and applied the teachings to my Private Group of past customers that was doing "ok" but not phenomenal. My business increased by 66%! I have had over 50 orders placed by past customers, 7 of them sent more than 1 referral that resulted in a sale, 10 past customers sent referrals that created new leads as future customers, and 2 new distributors! I had not seen numbers like this in my business over the 13 months prior to the book! What's more amazing is these numbers are from me resurrecting old customers! The possibilities are endless!"

— Nicole Hanson

25 new distributors in a month thanks to Network Marketing For Facebook!

"We joined our network marketing company simply to get our mojo back and look good for our wedding. Network Marketing For Facebook book taught us about the power of adding prospects to our Facebook Group. With this one strategy, we added an additional 25 distributors to our team last month."

— Michele Bundy and Jay O'Donnell

11 new customers and 2 distributors thanks to Network Marketing For Facebook!

"Using your private message education, I sent out 35 samples of my product. It turned into 11 new customers earning me $584 plus 2 new distributors! I started with 682 Facebook Friends and now have 855. Graph search connected me to 287 people using your interest list education and 78 of them are now friends."

– Bob Weiss

Increase of 6-14 samples given out monthly thanks to NMFF!

"Network Marketing for Facebook has been a great read! Because of it, I have had more interaction in my VIP group for my customers– they are LOVING my exclusive samples! Previously, I might get one or two people requesting samples. But now from the skills I have learned, I can get anywhere from 7-15 samples sent out every month! I have also been more confident in talking and building new relationships! I previously would only get responses from 3 people for every 5 I messaged and now it's turning into 5 out of 5 response rate! This book is a great read and I learn something new every time I've read it!"

– Caitlin Ruf

1 new customer and 2 new distributors thanks to Network Marketing For Facebook!

"I applied the private message strategy in the book. I sent 40 messages. 10% have not seen the message yet, 18% seen but not responded, 58% wanted more information & requested samples, and 15% not interested. Of those that requested samples (58%) 7 of the 23 are interested. One already enrolled as a customer and 2 enrolled as distributors."

– Shari Holliman-Ave Beesley

2 new customers and 10 more close to ordering thanks to Network Marketing For Facebook!

"Using what I learned in Network Marketing For Facebook, I've contacted, on average, 12 new people per day since April 15th, 2015. I now have 14 people in the next stage of learning about my business. These people I spoke to on the phone, they received an email and I have scheduled follow up calls with them. I signed up 2 new customers and have 10 more close to ordering. Awesome! Can you imagine if I had spoken to 30 new people per day as what is taught in the book?!"

– Jo Clark

6 people interested in my business and 5 meeting me for lunch thanks to Network Marketing For Facebook!

"I had 170 Facebook friends on April 20th when I read Network Marketing For Facebook. As of May 22nd, I now have 415. I averaged about 20% – meaning 1 in 5 accept my friend request. I do not personally know any of my new friends. I have just now started to see a response and my likes and comments on my posts are increasing. Right now, I have 6 people interested in my product and 1 interested in becoming a distributor. I am having great conversations with strangers on Messenger and it is awesome. I have plans to personally meet with 5 of them in the next 2 weeks. I figure since the people are strangers it took the month for people to see my posts, get to know me a little and now ask about my business."

– Janice Stein

4 new customers thanks to Network Marketing For Facebook!

"I sent 31 samples of my product after using the private message strategy taught in Network Marketing For Facebook. So far, 4 people purchased product from me!"

– Justina Friesen

2 new customers thanks to Network Marketing For Facebook!

"This week has been awesome! I applied your Facebook practices and acquired 64 new people of which 10 are definite prospects/customers. I sold a weight management pack, and signed up 1 other customer."

– Devorah McPherson

4 new customers thanks to Network Marketing For Facebook!

"Not the biggest sale of the week, but its the first leg of my journey. I have sold 2 canisters, as well as two bags of protein shakes. I have a customer who is excited to see what the product can do for her and she was so sweet. She said, 'If it helps me I know it can help others and then I want to get set up to be a distributor.' Network Marketing For Facebook works!"

– Amy Gibson Duncan

Reviews of The Workbook

Why a Network Marketing for Facebook Workbook? Because we need to stop reading and start doing. I like step-by- step actions steps. Action is what will get us results. Using proven techniques that work on Facebook to build real relationships is our number one strategy. And that is how to make Facebook a key part of your business-building portfolio. So don't just read this workbook. Use it!

- Tom "Big Al" Schreiter,
44 year network marketing legend, Fortune Now

———

Jim is so good and very thorough in his ability to show people how to harness the power of Facebook to grow their business. There is no way readers won't improve their prospecting and connecting if they implement this information.

- Brian Carruthers, Seven-Figure Income Earner in network marketing and Author of Building an Empire

———

This material will help you and your teams accomplish success faster. Jim, Marianne, and Brian have given you a simple, proven plan of action.
- Robert Butwin, Author, trainer, consultant

———

"Jim Lupkin is world-class at teaching how to successfully integrate the power of social media with the leverage of your network marketing business. The practical insights, hands-on exercises, and helpful tips covered in Jim's workbook will benefit network marketing professionals everywhere."

- Garrett McGrath, President of the Association of Network Marketing Professionals (ANMP)

———

"LOVE the workbook! Phenomenal, thought-provoking tool for the newest distributor to seasoned professionals! When used as part of a daily plan of action, this workbook can be an instrumental tool to help launch new distributors, shorten their learning curve, get and keep people engaged and connected, and increase retention, professionalism and success!"

- Babette Gilbert-Teno, Six-figure income earner in network marketing, Consultant Nutritionist to Reality TV, Speaker and Writer

———

"I thought you guys did a great job with Network Marketing for Facebook. However, diving into this new workbook puts the book into overdrive. The companies that embrace the book and workbook will truly have a leg up on lowering attrition and attracting new customers."

- Troy Dooly, Beachside CEO

———

"Network Marketing for Facebook is an exceptional read that includes extremely useful strategies for growing your business, including what many books lack: exercises to help you learn! Anyone wanting to get better at building on Facebook should be reading this and putting it to use."

- Todd Falcone, Author and Independent Network Marketing Trainer

———

"I highly recommend this workbook as a companion to Network Marketing for Facebook. Apply these practical and powerful insights, techniques, and tips, and grow your business through Facebook and beyond!"

- Valerie Bates, Author, Professional Networker, Business Coach

———

"The workbook companion to Network Marketing for Facebook encourages distributors to dig deeper into discovering their motivation and drive to be successful with their business. It also provides valuable activities to prepare the distributor to handle objections and to share their passion for their company, products, and goals. I highly recommend that both new and experienced distributors read Network Marketing for Facebook and use the companion workbook to boost their business and provoke action and thought. I look forward to sharing both of these books with my teams and challenging them to complete the entire workbook."

- Nichole Smith, Seven-figure earner with a team of 400,000 distributors

———

This writing team has created another amazing tool: the up, down, across, and sideways of using Facebook in network marketing. Wonderful insights and exercises will help readers truly "get it." Highly recommend!

- Andrea Waltz, Co-Author, Go for No!

———

"We started our network marketing business before social medial was introduced, so it's been a learning curve. NMFF has helped us integrate social media as part of our overall business strategy. We have increased our cycles and, recently, ranked advanced. We're extremely grateful to Jim, Marianne, and Brian for their training to help us implement these tips."

- Kathy and Carl LaMarr, Six-figure income earners in network marketing

———

"This workbook is a priceless resource that every distributor who wants to be relevant in today's marketplace should have their hands on! The key concepts, so simply and effectively taught, along with practical application steps, are critical for any network marketer to understand and adopt ... to not only become successful, but distinguished in their profession. I definitely feel this is the perfect curriculum to give my team a cutting-edge advantage. The workbook walks a distributor through practical information on developing vital people skills by complimenting classic approaches with modern-day techniques in a way that educates, empowers, and compels action. One of the things I like most is that this workbook is about expanding your professional ability and applying that finesse to Facebook to enhance your overall business strategy. It bridges the gap between real-life, human interaction and relationship building through social media."

- Nicole Wong, Multiple Six-Figure Income Earner in network marketing

———

"Living in a world where we are so connected virtually is a blessing AND a curse. I am 23 years old and understand that utilizing Facebook for business must be done right or not at all. It's difficult because there isn't a manual that shows us how to market our business, connect, and actually have success using Facebook (without sounding "salesy") Well, now there is! This book is a must read. I have and will continue to read it over and over again. Personally, I need a guide and workbook that involves thought in order to grow and learn, and this book does the trick! Thank you, Jim and Marianne Lupkin and Brian Carter for creating this effective, poignant, and sensational book!"

- Ashley Aliprandi, Author, Speaker, Life Coach

———

"The principles of building a network marketing business have never changed but technology has. Facebook is not going anywhere, and there are FEW quality resources on how to communicate with and use Facebook effectively. Jim has put together a comprehensive guide to learning the LANGUAGE of Facebook and using it as a strategy to COMPLIMENT an offline network marketing business. If you are building a network marketing business in the 21st century, you need this workbook."

- Hale Pascua Six-Figure Income Earner in network marketing

———

"This workbook is an amazing testament that you can learn how to take a high tech world and bring it into a high touch-recruiting model. What Jim and Marianne Lupkin and Brian Carter have put together is a recruiting masterpiece, as if you were talking to your friends and family all over the world. I really would suggest this workbook to anybody who is looking to build a successful network marketing business. I, myself, have you used these same techniques to build a very successful business. I even met my wife on Facebook, so I know a little something about recruiting on Facebook! Don't hesitate to get this workbook and take your business to another level."

- Joseph McDermott, Six-Figure Income Earner in network marketing

———

"Social media is a huge tool for network marketers. Jim Lupkin's book is a must-read if you're building your Network Marketing business, and the new Network Marketing For Facebook Workbook is a wonderful addition to Jim's top-selling book. I highly recommend every networker get a copy of both!"

- Amber Voight, Seven-Figure Income Earner, social media and network marketing coach

———

"Social media, especially Facebook, has changed the game for network marketers. I can't imagine building my business or my team culture without Facebook. But many are confused by these new tools that we have today and settle for being overwhelmed by it. There is, indeed, a lot to learn. Kudos to Jim and his team! I so appreciate that Jim and Marianne Lupkin and Brian Carter have created this incredible tool for our profession. This workbook will help you truly understand how to build your business using the best that social media and technology has to offer. I am excited to share this with my team!"

- Kathleen Deggelman, Six-Figure Income Earner in network marketing

TABLE OF CONTENTS

Introduction

To our network marketing friends,

Network Marketing For Facebook has been tremendously successful. Our book couldn't have reached that level without our dedicated readers – you. We understand what you go through on a daily basis to build your business because we did it ourselves. We know you have many options when choosing training materials and coaches to grow your business. Thank you for choosing us and giving us an opportunity to show you how you can be successful using Facebook. We appreciate you!

As of March 2016, *Network Marketing For Facebook* is available through 65 network marketing companies, representing more than 10 million distributors. The book has sold out at many company conventions, and 35,000 distributors follow the book on Facebook.

Some of the most well-respected publications in the network marketing profession, such as Inc., Direct Selling News, and Networking Times Magazine, wrote articles about the book. The book made the Top 25 Social Media Book To Read In 2015 list, a selection compiled by some of the world's greatest social media leaders and influencers.

Distributors around the world are realizing extraordinary success because of the principles found in *Network Marketing For Facebook*. Many distributors asked for more. More guidance. More insights. More of everything the book offered to those who are looking to grow their portion of the network marketing profession.

The *Network Marketing For Facebook Workbook* is for those who crave more.

Each workbook chapter corresponds to a chapter from *Network Marketing for Facebook*. Along with interactive activities such as true/false and multiple choices designed to test your understanding of our strategies, each chapter includes exercises to take that knowledge further than you ever thought possible. Each chapter also features Jim Lupkin's Insider Tips, exclusive content to help you translate your social media experience into success. Jim should know. Over the past twenty years, Jim has coached and trained over 100,000 distributors, producing sales of more than $100 million through social media.

What will you gain from actively engaging in this workbook?

- Knowledge Check gives you clarity, so you can put our *Network Marketing for Facebook* strategies to work
- Fill-in-the-Blank shows a picture of your existing business, so you know where you need to improve
- Did You Know provides a deeper insight into social media and network marketing, so others see you as an influencer
- Mental Check opens your mind, so you don't get in the way of your own success
- Insider Tip shortens your learning curve, so you can succeed in less time by knowing what the most successful distributors know
- Exercises puts your newfound knowledge into practice

Our team has put hundreds of hours into creating this workbook. However, achieving success is up to you. Anything worth doing takes time and commitment. Facebook is worth it. Use this workbook to build a team in your town before expanding nationally or internationally. Take ownership of the workbook by marking it up – scribble in the margins, highlight, dog-ear the pages. Working through a workbook is an interactive experience, and the physical process of writing your answers creates new memory pathways in the brain.

Let's get started!

Jim Lupkin, Marianne Lupkin and Brian Carter

Chapter 1

Facebook Is Part of the Strategy, Not the Whole Strategy

Why do some distributors struggle to find success on Facebook even though these distributors know every Facebook feature and how to use it for business? For the same reason distributors who have a great deal of product knowledge sometimes struggle within their company.

Facebook and product knowledge are only part of the strategy, not the whole strategy. It takes understanding and the application of a complete strategy to be successful in the network marketing profession.

Let's explore the whole strategy, so you can succeed on Facebook. Take a few minutes to reread or skim chapter two in *Network Marketing For Facebook* before completing this section.

Knowledge Check 1.1		
(Circle your answer)		
T	F	When you use only Facebook, the singular strategy will fail you, just as if you used only email to build your business.
T	F	There are enough features on Facebook for you to develop deep, meaningful relationships with those who eventually become customers or distributors on your team.

Fill In The Blank
Your Network Marketing WHY
Why did you join the network marketing profession?

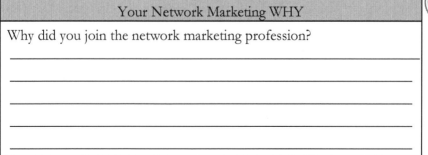

Let's dive deeper into your why by using the Onion Method. The Onion Method allows you to peel away your motivations until you find the deepest reasons for your actions and choices.

Here's an example of how it works:

- You want to earn $5,000 a month in your network marketing company. Why?
- Because you want to go part-time at your existing job. Why?
- Because you're working 60 hours a week and you want to spend more time with your family. Why?
- Your children are growing up fast, and quality time is at a premium. Why?
- Life is more than a job or making money. It's about spending quality time with your family. Why?
- (You can't come up with anything else, so you're done. You've reached the most fundamental why.)

As you can see, your why is bigger than just saying you want to earn $5,000 a month. Your why is time freedom—the freedom to share every precious moment with your family, to laugh and smile as your son or daughter takes his or her first walk or run, to spend quality moments with your spouse on memorable dates, adventures, and vacations.

When you understand your why, you'll never consider quitting the network marketing profession.

Using the Onion Method, write below why you joined the network marketing profession? Ask, "Why?" as many times as you can below.

Fill In The Blank Onion Method	
Why?	
Why?	
Why?	

18

Fill In The Blank (continued)
Onion Method

Why?	
Why?	

Is your answer different now than it was before?

Did You Know?
Knowledge Check

Knowing your original why is not always enough. Knowing your real why is a vital step to being successful on Facebook.

Insider Tip
The $50 Lesson: Who Determines Your Worth?

I asked you to share your why with me. I thought it would be appropriate to share my why with you.

My father taught me a $50 lesson when I was 21 years old.

I helped my father replace a barn roof in the middle of a hot and humid summer day. My hands burned from the chemicals found in the shingles. After eight hours of intense work, he handed me a $50 bill.

I said, "I just busted my butt, and all I get is $50!?"

He smiled and said, "Let this be a lesson. When you work for someone else, that person determines your worth. You have no say in the matter. And if you work for someone else, you always hit a ceiling on how much you can make. Work for yourself. Be an entrepreneur. There's no stopping you then."

A few months later, I enrolled in college, double-majoring in entrepreneurship and finance. I've been an entrepreneur ever since. When times get tough, and they do, I say, "Alright, Jim. Do you want someone to determine your worth, or do you want to fight through this obstacle and continue living your dreams?"

I still carry the $50 bill (printed in 1996) in my wallet to remind me of that day.

I love you, Dad. One of the best lessons you taught me.

Mental Check
The Impact of Your WHY

When you feel like it's no big deal to achieve your why, think of the following.

- What if? What if you don't achieve it? What if your why is to spend more time with your children instead of working 60 hours a week? What if you miss their most important experiences? What if they grow up thinking it's okay that you missed all those experiences?
- If you have a different why, what will you miss?
- Do you realize your decisions create a ripple effect for generations to come? Shouldn't you be the beacon of hope for you and your family?

Let's make sure you never forget your why:

Exercise
WHERE to Keep Your WHY

Write your why in a place where you will read it daily—in the bills portion of your wallet, on the outside of your lipstick tube with a Sharpie, beneath your favorite refrigerator magnet, on your bathroom mirror above where you shave, as a once-daily text from your cell phone's remind feature. Maybe even tattoo it on your forehead. Just kidding!

_____

_____

_____

_____

_____

By completing this exercise, you will become intimate with your why. Your why will become part of you. People will sense your drive and determination every time they are around you. When others know your real why on Facebook, they tend to have a stronger interest in becoming a distributor. They believe you can help them achieve their why, as well.

Have Passion for Your Profession

	**Knowledge Check 1.2** (Circle your answer)	

T	F	You can succeed in the network marketing profession with some luck, hard work, dedication, and one strong distributor on your team.
	a.	Which of the following is true? The network marketing profession is a pyramid scheme
	b.	The network marketing profession is part of the direct sales industry
	c.	Only people at the top make money
	d.	None of the above
	e.	All of the above

Fill In The Blank
Network Marketing is #1

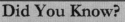

Explain why you think the network marketing profession is the best way for you to achieve success in today's world.

_____

_____

_____

_____

Did You Know?
Knowledge Check

As of 2015, more than 100 million worldwide network marketing distributors generate over $185 billion a year in sales.

Insider Tip
Network Marketing is a Valid and Valuable Profession

In October 1995, I became a distributor in the network marketing profession.

My best friend said, "Jim, this is the worst decision you've ever made!" He wasn't the only person who said that, either.

Another friend said, "Jim, haven't you heard my horror story of how my mom lost all her retirement money in one of those pyramid schemes? You're going to lose all your money, too!"

Insider Tip (continued)
Network Marketing is a Valid and Valuable Profession

After four months, I had yet to enroll one new distributor or customer. Part of my lack of success was the doubt my "friends" put in my mind.

Part of me said, "You can't trust this, Jim. Don't do it!"

But I decided to stay open-minded, learn the facts, and not listen to the ones who hadn't succeeded in network marketing.

A mentor told me, "This is a real profession where people really do succeed." I found out he was right.

Over the next four years in that company, I enrolled 40 distributors and had a team of 800 distributors around the United States.

The moral of the story? Be careful to whom you listen.

Mental Check
Network Marketing is On the Rise

Some of today's biggest brands use the network marketing profession, sometimes using the words *direct sales* or *affiliates*, to grow their business. These brands include Amazon, Netflix, Ebay and Direct TV, just to name a few.

The network marketing profession has also caught the attention of highly talented individuals with MBA degrees from colleges like Stanford and Harvard, as well as executives from companies like Coca-Cola and L'Oreal, to serve as executives for network marketing companies.

When you understand our profession, no matter what people say, you'll know you're in the right place.

Fill In The Blank
Be Ready To Stop The Critics

Write out a few responses so you're prepared to answer when a friend says, *"Is this a pyramid scheme?"* or *"This will never work!"*

Is this a pyramid scheme?	
This will never work!	

Insider Tip
Ask Questions Instead of Reacting

A great response starts with a question and continues with questions, so you can answer correctly. Think about the Onion method above.

Peel away layers by asking questions.

Here are two examples:

Example one:	Sarah says, *"Is this a pyramid scheme?"*
	Jim says, *"What do you mean?"*
	Sarah says, *"You know. One of those things where the person at the top makes all the money."*
	Jim says, *"That sounds terrible! This is definitely not a pyramid scheme. Everyone has the same opportunity to make as much money as they want, as long as they are willing to put in the time and effort. This holds true for anything you are doing, though, including your job. Can you imagine what would happen if you skirt by at your job and someone else puts in the time and effort? I would think they would pass you up for a promotion."*

|---|---|
<div align="center">**Insider Tip (continued)** Ask Questions Instead of Reacting</div>	
Example two:	Darren says, *"This will never work!"*
	Jim says, *"Why do you say that?"*
	Darren says, *"Because my friend joined a company like this, and she lost a lot of money."*
	Jim says, *"Do you know why she joined that particular company?"*
	Darren says, *"They promised she would get rich with very little effort."*
	Jim says, *"Why would she believe such a thing? You have to put in the time and effort to be successful at whatever you do in life. This profession isn't any different. Wouldn't you agree?"*
	Darren says, *"I guess so. Maybe you're right."*
	Jim says, *"If I were you, I would at least take a look at what I'm doing. You'll miss a lot of great opportunities with a closed mind."*

Exercise
Follow The Leaders

Let's make sure you have passion for your profession.

Write five credible network marketing associations, magazines, trainers, coaches, successful distributors, or influencers. Next, follow them on Facebook. Build your belief in the network marketing profession by reading their Facebook posts.

1. _____

2. _____

3. _____

4. _____

5. _____

By completing this exercise, you'll surround yourself with others who are passionate about network marketing. You become the people with whom you surround yourself. Passion is contagious. Showing your passion for the network marketing profession on Facebook instills belief in others who might not consider network marketing a viable option to making money.

Have Passion for Your Product and Network Marketing Company

Knowledge Check 1.3 (Circle your answer)			
T	F		You must believe you have the best products on the market (network marketing and non-network marketing products) for the quality and price.
T	F		You must believe you're in the best company for achieving your why.
			Which of the following demonstrates good practice?
		a.	Use the product every day
		b.	Give free samples to every friend
		c.	Stock the product in your home for those who live close to you
		d.	None of the above
		e.	All of the above
			To be passionate about your company, you should:
		a.	Work closely with someone who is earning a full-time income in the company
		b.	Attend local, regional, and national company events
		c.	Talk about all the problems the company is having with your team
		d.	a and b
		e.	All of the above

Fill In The Blank
Explore Your Passion

List five reasons why you think your product is the best in quality and price.	List five reasons why you think your company can help you achieve your why.
1. _____	1. _____
2. _____	2. _____
3. _____	3. _____
4. _____	4. _____
5. _____	5. _____

Did You Know?
Leaders Are Knowledgeable

Understanding your products and your company is the way to rise above 99% of the distributors in your company. Position yourself as a leader. Become informed.

Insider Tip
Know Your Product and Company

In 2001, I was a distributor for a network marketing company that promoted a nutritional supplement product. The company attracted tens of thousands of doctors and successful entrepreneurs. Why?

"We like the product quality," said the doctors.

"We wanted the opportunity to work with some of the most successful distributors in the profession," said the entrepreneurs.

I used the product every day to see my own body transformation. I studied the ingredients and the product competition.

I also educated myself on the training and compensation plan. I worked closely with the field leadership to learn how to be a network marketing professional.

My friends and acquaintances told me, "We feel your conviction, Jim. It's 100% clear you believe in this product and company."

I enrolled 500 distributors and generated millions of dollars in sales over a few short years. More importantly, those who also believed in the product and company noticed health benefits and made money.

Products: Your company may have many products. You may love some and not others. You can still do well without loving them all personally.

For example, you might say, "Hey, I'm a guy who sells skincare and cosmetics. I don't wear lipstick. How am I supposed to fall in love with the lipstick products?"

Because of this, you find yourself not talking about lipstick to potential customers, and this lowers your overall sales potential. The solution is to <u>use someone else's lipstick testimonial</u> to inspire someone to try it.

Network marketing company: You should believe your network marketing company will help you achieve your why. In order to have this belief, we suggest you focus in the following areas:

- The company owners
- The corporate team
- The leadership in the field
- The compensation plan

How do you get that belief? You study the areas above.

Listen to company calls to hear how the owner and corporate team handle themselves in front of distributors. Attend company events, and watch how the leadership in the field conducts themselves with the rest of the distributors. Study your compensation plan, as well as alternative plans in our profession.

If you don't study these essential aspects, you may find yourself joining many network marketing companies over the years but never achieving your why. Or worse, you might leave the profession.

Let's make sure you have passion for your products.

Use one of your products today. What did you like most about it?	
Write one statement that sets your product apart from the competition.	
Devote 15 minutes to studying your product's competition. Are your products competitive on quality and price?" Make notes here.	
Read customer testimonials on your company's Facebook Business Page and website today. What did you like the most about them? Jot one compelling testimonial here.	
List your product's ingredients. Be able to recall the most important ones from memory.	
Purchase your products top three competitors. Stage a head-to-head comparison for yourself or a select group of friends. Record their impressions as they compare.	

Exercise
Passion for Your Company

Let's make sure you have passion for your company.

Learn something new about your company by reading the company website today. Write three things that impress you from what you learned.	1. 2. 3.
Visit your company's Facebook Business Page and review what others say about the company. What three things did you like most from the feedback of others?	1. 2. 3.
Attend the next company conference call, webinar, or live event. Write three things you learned.	1. 2. 3.
Work with others who, like you, are driven by passion. Contact leaders above you, and work directly with them. The more you earn, the more they earn, so they should want to work with you personally. Name three top leaders with whom you would like to work.	1. 2. 3.

By completing these exercises, you'll gain a new appreciation for your products and company. This appreciation on Facebook shows confidence to your friends. They may ask about your business before you ask them.

People and Communication Skills

Knowledge Check 1.4		
(Circle your answer)		
T	F	People and communication skills are critical to the success of your business.
T	F	As long as people believe in your company and products, they will join your team as a distributor.
T	F	The ability to relate to others, knowing how and when to show empathy, and a genuine interest in others are all considered people skills.
T	F	Being personal, closed-minded, knowing what you're talking about, and speaking with clarity are considered communication skills.

Fill In The Blank
Know Your Strengths

List your three strongest people skills. Examples are: understanding different personality types, asking for feedback from others, giving quality feedback, influencing how others feel, and resolving conflicts quickly.

1. _____

2. _____

3. _____

List your three strongest communication skills. Examples are: understanding body language, being calm under pressure, and being an engaged listener.

1. _____

2. _____

3. _____

Did You Know?
How to Get What You Need with Communication

There are four parts to a whole communication message: facts, thoughts, feelings, and needs. What is objectively true? Facts. What are you thinking about it? Thoughts. What are you feeling about it? Feelings. What do you need as a result of this situation? Needs. When you aren't aware of all four communication elements and don't convey them all, people's response to you won't be as fulfilling.

For example, if you approach intellectual people with just your feelings and needs, they may think you're overreacting or that your needs don't make sense and aren't valid.

Similarly, if you approach people who are primarily emotional with just facts and thoughts, they may not feel moved by what you've said.

And even if you include everything else but needs, you'll find people understanding you but not giving you what you need. People are busy and overwhelmed. Connect the dots for them, or they may not get it.

Insider Tip
Improve Your Skills

Read books, listen to audio books, and attend online or off-line workshops, seminars, and conventions that teach these skills.

People Skills:	While you're improving, be aware that all personality types may not mesh with yours. That doesn't make those relationships any less valuable. If you meet an aggressive person who wants to look at your business but you feel intimidated, put him in contact with someone above you (sponsor) who is more experienced at dealing with that personality type. Instead of an awkward conversation that goes nowhere, the end result may be a new distributor on your team. Remember, your sponsor earns money when your team grows.
	One method I used to increase my people skills early in my network marketing career was to force myself to be around more people and learn through experience. I took a part-time job at a coffee shop meeting hundreds of new people every week. Within a short period of time, my skills increased exponentially. I made a lot of friends in the process.

Communication Skills:	While you are learning communication skills, avoid engaging in activities that hurt your business. For example, if you don't fully understand a communication skill like engaged listening, introduce your inquisitive friend to your sponsor, who is excellent at listening. Learn from watching your sponsor model that skill. One exercise you can do to practice engaged listening is listening 80% of the time while talking 20% in your next conversation with someone. The 20% should be you asking questions about what the other person is talking about. It's not as easy as it sounds because, by nature, we love to talk about ourselves. Have fun!
Communication Skills:	One method I used to increase my communication skills early in my network marketing career was doing part-time jobs that forced me to talk. One in particular, while I was in college, was a door-to-door sales job for Cox Cable. I canvassed neighborhoods in Rhode Island and Massachusetts, selling homeowners a free trial of bundled phone, cable and Internet services. It was scary. I felt uncomfortable talking to people about business. I had doors shut on me, stuttered when I spoke, and got lost with my words. After a while, the job became easier. I ended up being one of the top sales reps for the company out of 50 people.

Mental Check
Get Honest Feedback

Ask your friends, family, or trusted coworkers where you could improve on your skills. Their answers may surprise you. Be open-minded and remember you might not recognize your weaknesses. Their answers are gold, so be grateful. Be careful not to ask people who are emotionally abusive. Ask people who have a reputation for being objective.

Let's make sure you learn about people and communication skills.

Spend 10 minutes going to www.youtube.com and watching videos about people and communication skills. Share five things you learned from the videos.

1. _____

2. _____

3. _____

4. _____

5. _____

To further your knowledge, purchase a bestselling book about these skills. What book did you choose?

_____

To put your newfound knowledge to work, choose three friends. Teach them what you learned today. Which three friends did you choose?

    1. _____

    2. _____

    3. _____

By completing these exercises, you'll gain a better understanding of people and communication skills. Having strong people and communication skills on Facebook will allow you to cultivate many new Facebook friends and articulate your message in a way that will create an abundance of new customers and distributors.

Face-to-Face Time

		Knowledge Check 1.5
		(Circle your answer)
T	F	Your strongest Facebook relationships are friends you met face to face at some point.

Knowledge Check 1.5 (continued)
(Circle your answer)

		Which of the following is NOT a benefit of face-to-face communication?
	a.	You can see each other's facial expressions
	b.	You can see each other's gestures
	c.	You can add a personal touch by smiling
	d.	You can lose your prospects by spending too much time with one person face to face
	e.	None of the above

Fill In The Blank
Overcome Your Fears

If you're still resisting face-to-face meetings, write your fears:

_____

_____

_____

_____

Talk to your sponsor about these fears. Talking through your concerns may ease your anxieties. Your sponsor may have insights and experiences that will make a huge difference in your entire life, not just in network marketing.

Did You Know?
How In-Person Meetings Empower Social Media

Some people are nervous to meet in person. Facebook allows you to build rapport before meeting, making face-to-face time easier.

If you talk to your Facebook friends face to face, they will like, comment, and share your Facebook posts more often, as well as refer more friends to you for business.

Insider Tip
How to Make the Connection

After speaking with people face to face about your business, always send them a Facebook friend request. Since 1 out of 20 people join our profession as a distributor, doesn't it make sense to stay in touch with the other 19 until they are ready to become a distributor?

Here are the ways I'd approach someone:

- You don't have an opportunity to mention your business: During the conversation, make it a priority to learn her first and last name.

  Send her a Facebook friend request with a message on Facebook Messenger saying, "Hey! This is Jim. We met earlier today at our kids' soccer game. I really enjoyed our conversation, and I would love to be Facebook friends."

  After you become friends on Facebook, she'll learn about your business from your posts.

- Pain example: You visit a car dealership. During the sales process you say, "I'm amazed at your people skills. You're a great conversationalist. You must make a lot of money selling cars. Congrats!"

  He'll thank you and possibly tell you what he doesn't like about the job. He might say, "I do well here, but I work too many hours" or "I do well here, but I really don't make enough money." When you build up someone first, he is more likely to voice complaints about his job. If you try to tell him there is a better way immediately, he will often defend his job.

  Next, say, "I know someone who was just like you. She now makes a lot of money but doesn't work too many hours. I'd love to introduce her to you. Maybe she can help. How about I text you some information and friend you on Facebook?"

Mental Check
Why "No" Is Good

You may have a fear of rejection. Face to face is the most difficult way to hear someone say no to you about checking out your business.

Look at the word no as an opportunity. No means you're one step closer to a yes. More importantly, someone saying no has nothing to do with you. Your friend is saying no because she doesn't have an interest in your product or opportunity at this time.

Let's make sure you understand the power of face to face.

Today, set appointments to take three different distributors to lunch to celebrate a new customer or distributor on his or her team. Whom did you choose?

1. _____ 2. _____ 3. _____

Do you have a team outside your area? Schedule a Facebook Video Chat with three more distributors to celebrate their success. Whom did you choose?

1. _____ 2. _____ 3. _____

Celebrate the team's monthly accomplishments. Schedule a success dinner with all your local distributors at a local restaurant. Which three distributors can help you organize the dinner party?

1. _____ 2. _____ 3. _____

You have a phenomenal business in your hands that can change someone's life. Today, make three new face-to-face friends, and send these friends a friend request on Facebook. What are their names?

1. _____ 2. _____ 3. _____

We all have Facebook friends we haven't met face to face yet. Name three friends you would like to meet.

1. _____ 2. _____ 3. _____

By completing these exercises, you'll gain insight into how face to face strengthens your Facebook strategy. Don't think you can sit behind a computer and build a multi-million dollar network marketing business. Facebook success is built on relationships. Face to face is the strongest way to build concrete relationships that last a lifetime.

Phone Time

Knowledge Check 1.6
(Circle your answer)

T	F	Your friends don't need to hear your voice as long as you're speaking to them daily on Facebook.
T	F	Your voice is as unique as your fingerprints.

36

How many friends have you contacted on the phone, video chat, or voicemail through Facebook Messenger in the last seven days?

_____

Did You Know?
Two Critical Moments

On the phone, the first 30 seconds is crucial to establishing a positive perception about you through your voice and tone. The last 30 seconds is when a friend finalizes their opinion about your business.

Insider Tip
The 2,000 lb. Phone

It was Winter, 1995. My sponsor asked me to make a list of everyone I knew. After an 45 minutes of thinking, I came up with about 30 names.

Next, my sponsor asked me to call everyone on the list and ask them if they were open to a business opportunity. If they said yes or maybe, I would drop a VHS tape off at their house to review. If they liked what they watched, they may attend a weekly hotel meeting to meet others and receive a full presentation.

Gulp! I looked at the phone. I felt dizzy. The receiver weighed 2,000 pounds. I was sweating and nervous. Before anyone could pick up, I hung up. I paced back and forth. I couldn't do it.

Finally after 20 minutes, I made my first phone calls. Some said yes, and others said no. It wasn't as difficult as I thought it would be. There was something comforting about my friends and family hearing my voice.

Today, we can peak someone's interest on Facebook then text her to make sure she is available. By the time we connect on the phone, your friend is waiting for your call. People need to hear your voice!

With today's technology, you can do Facebook Video Chat and leave a voicemail on Facebook Messenger. The goal is for your connections to hear your voice so that you have a stronger emotional effect on them.

Mental Check
Just Do It. It Gets Easier

Do you find yourself sending a text message instead of making a phone call because you're nervous to talk with someone about your business? The more you speak on the phone, the easier it becomes. Repetition is the mother of success.

Exercise
I Can't Hear You!

Let's make sure you understand the power of voice.

Reach out to your team: Choose three people in your team with whom you haven't spoken on the phone. Reach out to them to say hello. Which three people did you choose?

1. _____ 2. _____ 3. _____

Phone time: Choose three people on your Facebook Friend List whose voice you haven't yet heard. Reach out to them on Facebook chat for a 10-minute conversation. Which three people did you choose?

1. _____ 2. _____ 3. _____

Voicemail time: Choose three people on your Facebook Friend List you consider to be real friends but with whom you aren't as close as you would like. Send them each a voicemail through Facebook Messenger. Which three people did you choose?

1. _____ 2. _____ 3. _____

By completing these exercises, you'll start to understand how your voice grows your business. Remember, it's always been about relationships. What's better than hearing your own voice? Hearing a friend's voice.

Attending Events

Knowledge Check 1.7
(Circle your answer)

T	F	Although company events are filled with excitement, most distributors leave events feeling discouraged because they are not as successful as others at the event.

38

T	F	Those who attend company events spend a lot of money without much return on their investment.
T	F	At company events, you'll develop friendships with people who are making it happen, which will make you a stronger leader.
		By attending company events, you can do the following:
	a.	Meet the owners of the company
	b.	Spend time with other distributors who are successful
	c.	Create an emotional connection with the company
	d.	None of the above
	e.	All of the above

Fill In The Blank
Your Convention Experiences

In your own words, write how you felt when you attended a company convention.

_____

_____

_____

_____

_____

Did You Know?
The LIVE Difference

Those who attend events become the most successful distributors in your company.

Watching videos and listening to calls are great, but until you get to live events, you won't *feel* the excitement. Without being emotionally connected to your company and its people, you'll never have the belief for your product or company like someone who attends live events.

Attending company events allows you to share those experiences on Facebook through images and videos. These shared experiences motivate your friends to become customers and distributors.

Most companies have local, regional and national events. Make it a point to attend each type of event, as they provide different experiences. For example, a local event might introduce you to the most successful distributors in a specific area, giving you confidence that you made the right decision to be a distributor. A regional event might introduce you to the VP of Sales for your company and 1,000 other distributors, giving you the fire to work even harder in your business. National events often put you in front of the company's owners and tens of thousands of distributors, giving you the unshakable belief you are in the right profession to make this a long-term career.

I attended my first local, 100-attendee event in Pottsville, Pennsylvania. I left the event energized and felt my life was about to change. The speaker was everything I wanted to be, and the crowd was full of positivity.

About a year later, I attended my first regional event in Cherry Hill, New Jersey. About 1000 distributors were in attendance. The event required four hours of total drive time, so I carpooled with a friend to save on gas money. I left the event thinking this opportunity was so much bigger than I thought, and I couldn't miss out on it.

Soon after, I attended my first national convention in Philadelphia, Pennsylvania. I didn't have much money, so I shared a hotel room with five other people. I walked into the building, and there must've been more than 20,000 distributors, screaming and dancing. That weekend, I met the owners and the most successful distributors company-wide. I left that national event a changed man. I believed nothing was impossible and, without a doubt, I was going to be a successful entrepreneur in the network marketing profession.

Mental Check
Event Attendance Obstacles

We all have obstacles when attending events. Two simple steps can help you identify these obstacles.

First, identify the obstacle. If you don't know the true nature of a problem, you can't fix it. Next, check your attitude. An obstacle cannot be overcome unless you have a clear mind. Don't allow yourself to become frustrated.

Make smart decisions. Cancel your cable for a few months to save money. Bring a babysitter along to help with your child. Carpool to save gas money.

There is a solution for every problem. Be creative.

Exercise
Just Go!

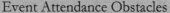

Let's make sure you understand the power of events.

- What is the date for your next local event? Start making plans to attend. _____

- What is the date for your next regional event? Start making plans to attend. _____

- What is the date for your next national event? Start making plans to attend. _____

What are the top five obstacles preventing you from attending events?

1. _____

2. _____

3. _____

4. _____

5. _____

By completing these exercises, you'll set yourself up to attend your company events. Realize that attending even one event can make the difference between success and failure in this business.

Handing Out Samples (if applicable)

Knowledge Check 1.8
(Circle your answer)

T	F	By sending out samples, you let the product do the selling for you.

Fill In The Blank
Put Yourself In Their Shoes

Did you try a sample before joining as a distributor? If so, write about how it felt to sample the product for the first time. How did your impression change over time as you became more familiar with the product.

_____

_____

_____

_____

Did You Know?
Get Their Info

In order for samples to be a successful marketing tool, collect the contact information of the person receiving the sample. Success happens in the follow up.

Insider Tip
Why Samples?

Sampling allows you to build long-term, residual income because others fall in love with the product and re-order year after year. What's the total cost to send one sample?

Understanding the cost allows you to know how many you can afford to give away each month. If you're unsure of the cost, get in touch with those who earn a full-time income in your company to find out.

After you send out 100 samples, do the math. Figure out how many samples it takes for you to acquire 1 new customer. Next, ask your company, "How many samples do I need to send out for 1 new customer?" If the answer is 1 out of 5 and you are doing 1 out of 15, make adjustments. Maybe you are sending out the wrong type of samples. Perhaps your friends need to see a company video, customer testimonials, or another marketing piece before you send a sample.

If your company doesn't sample, skip this step. Instead, have interested friends read company literature to build their belief in your product and business. This will give them the confidence to pay to try the products, especially if you offer them a money-back guarantee. If you don't have a money-back guarantee, use the power of social proof to build confidence in your potential customers.

Mental Check
Fear of Spending Money on Samples

Imagine opening a bakery. Wouldn't you let new customers sample your cupcakes? If they loved the taste of the cupcakes, they'd place an order. This method is more likely to lead to a sale than showing ingredients and packaging. Sampling is the quickest way to convert someone to a customer because, by nature, humans purchase based on emotion and experience, not logic and theory. "This cupcake tastes amazing," is always going to generate more sales than, "Cupcakes in general are good, and this appears to be a cupcake."

Exercise
Know It Backwards and Forwards

Let's make sure you understand samples.

Write the details of your sample program. Memorize it so that others know how easy it is to try your products.

_____

_____

_____

_____

_____

If you don't have a sample program, write the details of your money-back guarantee. Others will know they have nothing to lose by trying your products.

_____

_____

_____

_____

_____

If you don't have a money-back guarantee, write three resources you can share with your friends so they have confidence your products work.

1. _____

2. _____

3. _____

By completing this exercise, you'll be successful sending samples, explaining a money-back guarantee, or sharing resources to help motivate people to become customers or distributors. The most powerful tool you have in your network marketing company is the product. Share the products correctly, and watch your business grow quickly.

Personal Development

		Knowledge Check 1.9 (Circle your answer)
T	F	Personal development helps you believe in yourself and grow as a person.
	a. b. c. d. e.	Which of the following are true? Personal development only works for younger people Personal development happens between the ears Personal development helps you break through mental blocks b and c All of the above

Fill In The Blank
Bookworms Win

List the titles of books you have read and events you have attended in the last year for personal development. What did you learn from those efforts listed?

Books/Events	What You Learned
_____	_____
_____	_____
_____	_____
_____	_____
_____	_____

Did You Know?
Grow More to Earn More

$500 million is spent on personal development products every year.

If you've only made $50,000 a year for the last 20 years, you'll need to grow as a person to earn $120,000.

Most believe that personal growth is the number one ingredient for success.

Did You Know? (continued)
Grow More to Earn More

Many people who don't succeed on Facebook, in network marketing, in business, and even in their personal life, fail because they have a mental block.

Having a foundation of personal development in your life allows you to help other Facebook friends when you see them struggling with everyday issues. Reaching out builds relationships. In turn, friends may turn into customers and distributors.

Insider Tip
Personal Development

I understood the power of personal development early in my network marketing career because of the importance put on it by my first company.

I made a commitment to learn everything I could about the subject. I read 20 minutes a day, 7 days a week. I've read more than 52 books about personal development. Did you know a Ph.D. degree requires you to read 52 books on a particular subject then write a thesis on it? I guess I have my Ph.D. in personal development. I encourage you to do the same.

Having a strong personal foundation is one of the reasons I refused to quit during the toughest obstacles and challenges of my 20-year network marketing career.

Mental Check
How to Find More Time

Too busy to read personal development books? Try the following.

Listen to personal development audio books while you are driving to work or in the shower. Watch personal development videos on YouTube or Facebook while cooking or just before bed.

Make time for personal development. Everyone is busy. It's about priorities. What's important to you? Your business won't grow if you don't grow.

| **Exercise** |
| Get Specific |

Let's make sure you have personal growth in your own life.

List five personal development books you would like to read, including the cost. Purchase them today.

       Book Name   Cost Estimate

1. _____

2. _____

3. _____

4. _____

5. _____

List three personal development events you would like to attend, including the cost. Make plans to attend.

       Event Name   Cost Estimate

1. _____

2. _____

3. _____

Write five people of influence whom you would like to emulate. Put these five people in a Facebook Interest list and follow their words of inspiration on Facebook.

1. _____

2. _____

3. _____

4. _____

5. _____

Starting today, make it a priority to teach your team what you learn during your personal development journey. Create three-minute, topical selfie videos then post the videos in your Facebook Group to inspire your team. Make a commitment now when you will post your first video.

First Video Post Date: _____

By completing these exercises, you'll not only start your personal development journey, but your distributors will gain from your newfound knowledge. Many successful distributors believe network marketing is a personal development journey with a compensation plan. If you grow, your check grows.

Work the Numbers

Knowledge Check 1.10
(Circle your answer)

T	F	On average, you'll enroll one new distributor for every 20 people who look at your business.
	a.	Which of the following are true? Knowing the numbers eases your frustration
	b.	Numbers are the same for every company when enrolling distributors
	c.	Numbers are not important
	d.	All of the above
	e.	a and b

Fill In The Blank
Now You

What numbers have you experienced in your network marketing career?

_____

Did You Know?
The Reality of the Numbers

Out of 20 people who join your business, one will achieve his or her financial goal. For example, if you speak to 500 people about your business and 25 enroll as a distributor, one out of the 25 will work hard enough to achieve his or her financial goal.

It's easy to become frustrated if the first 15 people say no to your business, especially if they were all friends and family. You might question if you have what it takes. This doubt might be strong enough to make you quit. However, when you understand the true numbers of successful network marketing, you know this degree of rejection is normal. Understanding the numbers prevents frustration.

Understanding the numbers allows you to fully appreciate Facebook Graph Search and the immense opportunity it provides for your network marketing business.

When you understand the numbers, you can't blame others for your failure. Numbers set you up for success because you'll know how many people you need to speak with in order to achieve your why.

I remember when I was taught the numbers. My friend, Mark Yarnell, was in my upline in the early 2000s. He was my friend, coach, and mentor. Sometimes, I'd find myself chatting with him at 2 a.m. He was filled with endless stories and inspiration.

One night, I asked him, "Why do people say no? This is an amazing opportunity and product."

Mark replied, "Don't worry about who says yes or no. After making a couple hundred thousand dollars a month in my last company and interviewing many distributors who've earned $100,000 a month or more, I've come to a conclusion. For every twenty people you speak with, only one is going to enroll as a distributor. Out of every twenty people you enroll as a distributor, only one is going to become a strong and influential leader. If you focus on the numbers, you will easily hit whatever income you desire. Stay focused on talking to new people, and don't get hung up on those who say no. You can't beat the numbers."

I wondered if it was that easy. After that phone conversation, I left Mark a voicemail every day saying, "Hey, Yarnell, I spoke to (X) people today. Just keeping you in the loop. Bye!"

The numbers were true. I enrolled 500 distributors in that company by speaking to 10,000 people. Twenty-five distributors who enrolled became strong, influential leaders.

Don't doubt the numbers. If you are not getting these numbers, perhaps you need to improve another part of the strategy, like people and communication skills.

Mental Check
Expand Instead of Micromanaging

You may feel like you should be motivating your team more than enrolling new distributors. Remember that you can't want success more than someone else wants it for himself or herself. Many distributors spend time micromanaging their team when they should be enrolling new distributors. Your team will do as you do, not as you say. Start enrolling and watch your team explode!

Let's make sure you work the numbers.

For every 20 people with whom you speak, one should enroll as a distributor. Track your numbers by using pen and paper, a note app on your phone, or Excel on your computer. Count everyone. Did you just ask the waitress and she said no? You may not know her name but she counts! Mark her down as *Applebee's waitress*. This is a great way to see exactly how you are doing in the business. After a few hundred people, you should notice one out of 20 becomes a distributor. Write the last 10 people with whom you spoke about your business.

_____ _____ _____ _____ _____

_____ _____ _____ _____ _____

Out of every 20 distributors on your team, one should aggressively work the business with you. Review your team today. Determine if you are doing better, the same, or worse than the industry average by filling in the blank below.

I have _____ out of every 20 distributors on my team working the business aggressively.

By completing these exercises, you'll gain an appreciation for the numbers. Once you become committed to the numbers, this endeavor becomes a real business instead of an emotional one that you want to quit every other week because you think no one is interested.

Final Thoughts

Do you believe Facebook is part of your strategy, not the whole strategy?

Without passion, people and communication skills, face to face and phone time, attending company events, handing out samples, mastering personal development, and understanding the numbers, Facebook will only take you so far.

If you can apply the whole strategy, Facebook will allow you a platform where you never run out of people to speak with about your business. You'll always have opportunities to build strong relationships with current customers, distributors, and friends who could be the next distributor to join.

What are your five biggest takeaways from this chapter?

1. _____

2. _____

3. _____

4. _____

5. _____

NOTES:

Chapter 2

Why You Should Use Facebook

I magine you had the opportunity to attend two meetings in your area. In one meeting, you would be able to share your business with 50 people. In the other, 250 people will be in attendance. Which would you choose?

Take a few minutes now to reread or skim chapter three in *Network Marketing For Facebook* before completing this workbook section.

Knowledge Check 2.1		
(Circle your answer)		
T	F	You would be more successful attending a meeting of 50 people because it's more intimate than being in a crowd of 250.
T	F	I don't need to have a good relationship with someone in order for him or her to be my customer or join as a distributor in my business. The product and opportunity sells itself.
		What is the key to long-term success in the network marketing profession?
	a.	Knowing every detail of your compensation plan
	b.	Understanding every product ingredient in your product line
	c.	Having quality relationships with your friends, customers, and distributors
	d.	None of the above
	e.	All of the above

Fill In The Blank
Know, Like & Trust

People order products and build business with those they know, like, and trust. In your own words, describe what the following three words mean to you.

Know:

_____

_____

Like:

_____

_____

Trust:

_____

_____

Do you believe Facebook will help grow your business? Why or why not?

_____

_____

Did You Know?
Facebook Is The World

Most of your friends are already using Facebook for personal reasons, like connecting with friends and family.

On August 24th, 2015, Facebook made history when one billion people used Facebook in a single day. This means one in seven people on Earth used Facebook to connect with their friends and family in a 24-hour period.

Insider Tip
Facebook Wins Social Media

Nine years before Facebook launched, I used social media to grow my network marketing business. Yes, this medium of connection has been around long before the media decided to call it social media.

In the late 1990's, I used AOL and Yahoo Chat Groups to find new customers and distributors on the Internet. At any given time, I entered a chat group with 200 entrepreneurs and spoke about my business.

In the early 2000s, the Internet went from being a tool primarily used to search for information, like Google, to being a tool to facilitate communicate with others in a far more complex way than traditional chat rooms. Blogging launched. Soon after, social networking became popular.

The media loves to name things, so they called this new Internet Web 2.0.

Blogging did well, but people seemed to like social networking sites more. Friendster and MySpace were two of the early social networking sites. With network marketing, I leaned toward social networking sites as well.

I went from a chat room of 200 potential business prospects to tens of thousands every time I logged into MySpace. Blogging didn't offer these types of numbers without a lot of hard work.

Facebook was founded in 2004. In 2005, MySpace sold for more than $500 million dollars.

Once again, the media had to come up with a name other than what had come before because Web 2.0 wasn't sexy enough. What was sexy? Social media.

Once MySpace sold, a frenzy of entrepreneurs who wanted to create the next MySpace spawned. Thousands of social networking sites were born. I also joined in on the frenzy and co-created my own social networking site to compete against other social networking sites, like Facebook. Our site was created to connect network marketing professionals and entrepreneurs. It became the 17,000th most visited website out of 85 million websites in the world at the time. While Facebook was focused on offering their social network to students with a college email address and employees with a company email address, other social networks found their market share catering to specific topics and populations.

It was an exciting time! In the end, most social networks went out of business. People grew tired of being part of so many different websites. Only a handful survived, and today, only a few are even worth talking about.

Facebook is the clear winner in social networking, now called Social Media.

Mark Zuckerberg, co-founder of Facebook, once said in an article that his passion is to connect the world. He has a passion bigger than money. I believe his passion is the reason no other social media site has come close to competing with Facebook.

Facebook continues to push the limits. They invested resources into being a mobile-friendly website. They added video to their platform and, within 12 months, surpassed YouTube's success. They are aggressive in pursuing new technologies, like virtual reality with their purchase of Oculus and the Internet.org campaign, designed to connect people in third-world countries to the Internet.

It's hard to beat a company when you have this much passion behind it.

I've used nearly every social media site to build contacts in the network marketing profession. None came close to the results I get with Facebook.

In our profession, most distributors quit if they haven't earned money within 90 days. New distributors will stay on your team (downline) for years to come if they can earn a few hundred dollars a month. Doesn't it make sense to focus on sites like Facebook, where you can meet the most people and have plenty of opportunities to build relationships with them in the shortest period of time? You have 90 days to impact a new distributor on your team. Why not optimize a new distributor's chance of success by utilizing the most successful social media in the world?

Mental Check
Winners Use The Most Powerful Tools of The Day

You may feel uncertain if Facebook can help you succeed in the network marketing profession. Change is never easy.

Mental Check (continued)
Winners Use The Most Powerful Tools of The Day

In the 1990's, successful distributors used VHS and cassette tapes to pique the interest of their friends. Whiteboards became a slick new way to give presentations so that friends could decide if they want to be a customer or distributor.

In the early 2000's, successful distributors replaced VHS and cassette tapes with DVDs. PowerPoint presentations replaced whiteboard sessions.

After a few years, online presentations and videos replaced DVDs and PowerPoint slides.

Online communication continued to push boundaries. Conversations via computer became as commonplace as face to face or phone. Social networks (social media sites) evolved so that you could effectively introduce your business to someone online and she would enroll as a customer or distributor before meeting with you face to face or on the phone.

Why have distributors continued to use the latest in tools and communication to build their business? Simply said, better communication builds better network marketing businesses.

Facebook has remained strong in the social media landscape. With more than one billion people using it every day, it's so much more than someone posting what he ate for dinner.

Change is never easy. Look at the past to make the right decision on how to move forward.

Exercise - Part 1
You & Social Media

Reflect on what sites you are currently using for personal and business use. Using the lines below, share why you use the site and what you like and dislike about the site.

Facebook:	Why: _____
	Like: _____
	Dislike: _____

Exercise - Part 1 (continued)
You & Social Media

Twitter:	Why: _____
	Like: _____
	Dislike: _____
LinkedIn:	Why: _____
	Like: _____
	Dislike: _____
YouTube:	Why: _____
	Like: _____
	Dislike: _____
Instagram:	Why: _____
	Like: _____
	Dislike: _____
Other:	Why: _____
	Like: _____
	Dislike: _____

Exercise - Part 2
Your Friends & Social Media

Repeat the same exercise above for a few of your closest friends. Using the lines below, share why your friends use the site and what your friends like and dislike about the site.

Facebook:	Why: _____
	Like: _____
	Dislike: _____
Twitter:	Why: _____
	Like: _____
	Dislike: _____

Exercise - Part 2 (continued)	
Your Friends & Social Media	
LinkedIn:	Why: _____
	Like: _____
	Dislike: _____
YouTube:	Why: _____
	Like: _____
	Dislike: _____
Instagram:	Why: _____
	Like: _____
	Dislike: _____
Other:	Why: _____
	Like: _____
	Dislike: _____

By completing this exercise, you'll become aware of how you and your friends use some of the most popular social media sites for personal and business use. Your findings may surprise you. Ultimately, you have limited time when building your business. Focus your time where you connect with the most people, while building the strongest relationships.

Facts About Facebook

Knowledge Check 2.2	
(Circle your answer)	
	Which of the following are true about Facebook Profiles:
a.	You can show your personality
b.	You can share your photos, work history, and more
c.	Others can see a timeline of your life on Facebook
d.	Friends can fill out a contact form to learn about your business
e.	None of the above
f.	a, b, & c

Which of the following are NOT true about the Facebook Newsfeed:

a. You can interact with others
b. You can see what your friends are posting
c. You can poke someone
d. You can see a friend's Facebook Profile "About" section
e. None of the above
f. c & d

Facebook Graph Search:

a. Shows you a limited amount of people to speak with about your business
b. Connects you to people using search phrases
c. Shows mutual connections you have with people
d. Allows you to search for animals available for sale
e. None of the above
f. a & d

Which of the following are NOT true about Facebook Messenger:

a. You can video chat using Messenger
b. You can make phone calls by paying a low per-minute fee using Messenger
c. You can share your messages from Messenger in your newsfeed
d. You can have one-on-one conversations with others
e. None of the above
f. b & c

Photos and videos on Facebook:

a. Show the ingredients of your products in a pleasant visual layout
b. Capture the excitement of a distributor testimonial
c. Capture emotions that words can't
d. Show a story of your business
e. None of the above
f. All of the above

Which of the following are NOT true about your company Facebook Business Page:

a. Allows friends to interact directly with your company
b. Helps you become an expert on your products
c. Frees you to focus on your relationships with your friends
d. Creates social proof
e. None of the above
f. All of the above

A Facebook Group:

a. Creates social proof
b. Shows what it would be like as a distributor before joining
c. Gives access to support Monday – Friday
d. Creates a public space where anyone on Facebook can talk about your business
e. None of the above
f. c & d

Which of the following are NOT true about Facebook Events:

a. Give you an opportunity to meet with people face to face
b. Empower you to invite friends to local, regional, and national meetings
c. Let you invite friends to local get-togethers
d. Help you spam your friends
e. None of the above
f. All of the above

Facebook Save:

a. Helps you grow in personal development
b. Increases your communication skills
c. Increases your people skills
d. Grows your knowledge on your products and the network marketing profession
e. None of the above
f. All of the above

Fill In The Blank
Facebook Features

Which Facebook feature do you enjoy the most and why?

_____

_____

_____

_____

Did You Know?
Facebook Accelerates Network Marketing

In the 1990s, it took up to six days before someone would enroll as a distributor because of weekly hotel presentations.

In the early 2000s, it took someone only a few days to enroll as a new distributor thanks to the introduction of email and online presentations.

In 2015, someone can enroll as a new distributor in a few short hours thanks to Facebook.

Insider Tip
Network Marketing In Just 2 Fun Hours a Day With Facebook

If I were a distributor today in the network marketing profession, here's how I would use Facebook features.

Instead of reading the newspaper, magazines, watching the news on TV, searching Google, or listening to the radio in the morning, I would open Facebook Save on my phone and digest the news. I would spend 20 minutes learning about personal development, people and communication skills, leadership skills, information about my product, and worldly news that makes me more intelligent in conversation.

I would take 15 minutes of my day and use Facebook Graph Search to connect with 10 new friends. I would choose people in my local area so I have the opportunity to do lunch with them in the future.

Next, I would take a few minutes and use a photo or video to show off how I'm feeling at the moment so all my Facebook friends can see what I am up to.

Of course, I would return the favor by spending 10 minutes in my Facebook Newsfeed, liking and commenting on what my friends are doing, as well. A balance of give and take makes for a healthy relationship.

Insider Tip (continued)
Network Marketing In Just 2 Fun Hours a Day With Facebook

As I'm sampling my product through Facebook Messenger for 20 minutes, a few people tell me they love the sample they received last week and would like to be a customer. Before taking the order, I ask them if they want to earn extra money by handing out samples as well.

Some say, "Sure!"

I point them to the appropriate Company Facebook Page and Facebook Group for more information. I'd also ask them to check out the "About" section on my Facebook Profile to learn more about my background and what I'm doing. I'd schedule a phone call to connect with them later that day. The call might go well enough that they are ready to enroll. Because I used Facebook correctly, my call only lasted 20 minutes.

I might say, "Before you enroll, check out my Facebook Party tonight, using Facebook Events It's only 30 minutes. I want you to see how it's done before you commit. This is a party I'm doing with a friend who is not interested in being a consultant. She invited friends to check out the samples, and I'll be giving her free product in exchange. Right now, she has eight friends showing up. We are all going to be sitting in front of our computer, discussing the products and business."

I spent two, stress-free hours building my business this day.

Mental Check
Facebook Builds Teams

It takes more than you to create a full-time income in the network marketing profession. It requires building a team of distributors. Most of your distributors are on Facebook. Doesn't it make sense to learn Facebook to empower your team?

Exercise
Give Facebook a Real Try

Let's make sure you believe in Facebook.

Spend 10 minutes with FB Profiles today. Write your impressions/frustrations/anything new you learned.

_____

_____

Spend 10 minutes with FB Newsfeed today. Write your impressions/frustrations/anything new you learned.

_____

_____

Spend 10 minutes with FB Graph Search today. Write your impressions/frustrations/anything new you learned.

_____

_____

Spend 10 minutes with FB Messenger today. Write your impressions/frustrations/anything new you learned.

_____

_____

Spend 10 minutes on FB looking at photos and videos today. Write your impressions/frustrations/ anything new you learned.

_____

_____

Spend 10 minutes on your company's Facebook Business Page today. Write your impressions/ frustrations/anything new you learned.

_____

_____

Spend 10 minutes on your company's Facebook Group today. Write your impressions/ frustrations/anything new you learned.

_____

_____

Spend 10 minutes with FB Events today. Write your impressions/frustrations/anything new you learned.

_____

_____

Spend 10 minutes with FB Save today. Write your impressions/frustrations/anything new you learned.

_____

_____

Ask five (5) successful distributors in your company about their Facebook use today. Record new ideas to use Facebook effectively.

Distributor 1 (Name:_____) Tips:_____

Distributor 2 (Name:_____) Tips:_____

Distributor 3 (Name:_____) Tips:_____

Distributor 4 (Name:_____) Tips:_____

Distributor 5 (Name:_____) Tips:_____

By completing these exercises, you'll have a deeper appreciation for what Facebook can do to help you succeed in the network marketing profession. Those who understand and know how to use a product thoroughly always appear as a professional. Become a Facebook professional and watch your business soar.

Final Thoughts

Do you believe you should use Facebook?

Without understanding how social media evolved over the past 20 years, Facebook may not seem important.

If you believe in Facebook, your mind is probably swirling with possibilities of how it can help you achieve success in network marketing.

Out of more than a billion people on Facebook, you can easily find some who will love your products. Whether you are looking to build your business in your own backyard or share it around the world, Facebook is the perfect destination—a destination that allows you to meet unlimited amounts of people and build impeccable relationships with them, if you are willing to put in the time and effort.

What are your five biggest takeaways from this chapter?

1. _____

2. _____

3. _____

4. _____

5. _____

NOTES:

Chapter 3

Groups: Support Is Just A Few Clicks Away

What would you do if you were supported in your network marketing business 24 hours a day, seven days a week from thousands of other distributors in your company?

You would achieve success years faster by shortening your learning curve.

Let's learn how Facebook Group grows your business!

Take a moment now to refresh your knowledge of chapter four in *Network Marketing For Facebook*. Then complete this workbook section.

		Knowledge Check 3.1 (Circle your answer)
T	F	Being supported by others when you need help is one of the best ways to achieve success in network marketing.
		What does support look like in the network marketing profession?
	a.	Feeling excited? Share it so others are lifted up.
	b.	Feeling discouraged? Share it so others lift you up.
	c.	Have questions? Ask so you can move forward in your business.
	d.	None of the above
	e.	All of the above

Fill In The Blank No Man Is An Island
Have you experienced a time in your life when you felt discouraged and had no support system to help you through it? Write about that experience:
_____
_____
_____
_____

Fill In The Blank (continued)
No Man Is An Island

Have you experienced a time in your life where you had a support system? How did it make you feel? What was the outcome? Write about that experience:

_____

_____

_____

_____

Did You Know?
Whoa...

850 million people use Groups on Facebook.

Insider Tip
Reaching Up

Many distributors in our profession don't reach out to upline individuals who are earning a full-time income because they believe those people are too busy or they aren't successful enough to get the sponsor's attention. Remember, your sponsor earns money if you succeed. They want to hear from you. And, it feels good to help other people. Don't deprive them of the chance to be helpful and feel good.

I was fortunate to be trained and coached by Mark Yarnell.

For those who don't know Mark, here is a short bio:

Over a 29-year career in network marketing Mark Yarnell earned a reputation as one of the most passionate and respected advocates of the profession. Mark was an accomplished author and international business leader.

As a distributor, Mark developed an international organization of more than 300,000 distributors in twenty-one countries.

He published 11 books, including bestselling book *Your First Year in Network Marketing*.

Mark was the first and only person from networking marketing to serve as Contributing Editor to *Success Magazine*. He and Dr. Charles King of Harvard University co-created the first certification course in Network Marketing taught at the University of Illinois, Chicago, from 1993 – 2011. He was named the Greatest Networker in the *World by Upline Magazine* and indoctrinated into the Network Marketing Hall of Fame.

Over the course of three years, Mark taught me more about network marketing than anything I've learned in the other 17 years I've been in this profession.

Many people believe I've been successful because of social media alone. The truth is I've been successful because I gracefully combined Mark's teachings with social media.

Before working with Mark, I was in a company for four years, personally enrolled 40 distributors, and built a team of 800 distributors. Within three years working with Mark, I personally enrolled 500 distributors and created millions of dollars in sales.

One time, Mark traveled to Arkansas to help his father build a network marketing business. It went very well, and Mark left the state to open up other markets. By the time he traveled back to Arkansas, most of his father's team had fallen apart. Mark learned you can't build someone's business for him. You have to let the person lead and be there for support. He loved his family so much, he thought he was doing the right thing. This story was a wonderful lesson to me.

Find a trainer and coach. Learn everything from her and watch your business soar.

Thanks to Facebook Groups, it's easier today to work with these highly successful distributors, even if you are deep in their organization.

Mental Check
Success Is Social

You've been an employee your entire life. Now you've been given the opportunity to work for yourself in the network marketing profession. Consider the following.

Mental Check (continued)
Success Is Social

In a traditional workplace, most employees figure out things on their own because they compete against each other for pay raises and promotions. The idea of helping each other when you have 10 employees gunning for one open position is not ideal.

In the network marketing profession, the opposite is true. The more people help each other, the more everyone becomes successful. Receiving support from those who are successful in your company is paramount to your success. Few distributors in our profession have become successful without support.

Exercise
Learn Faster By Learning Other People's Lessons

Contact someone in your upline who is earning a full-time income in your company. Let him know you're serious about becoming a network marketing professional, and you'd love to have his full support. He should be happy to take you under their wing and mold you into a successful distributor. A great first question to ask is, "What obstacles did you overcome to get to where you are today?" Write notes regarding that conversation so you don't forget what you learned.

_____

_____

_____

_____

_____

_____

By completing this exercise, you'll gain access to some of the strongest support inside your company. Having the right person in your corner, training and coaching you every step of the way, will eliminate most failure.

Why Facebook Messenger and Facebook Pages Aren't Good Enough

Knowledge Check 3.2
(Circle your answer)

T	F	Facebook Messenger can't scale with your success.
T	F	Facebook Pages are a great way to build your business without spending money.

Fill In The Blank
Facebook Messenger & Pages

Do you currently use Facebook Messenger or Facebook Pages to support your team? What obstacles do you encounter? What do you like the most about these two features?

_____

_____

_____

_____

_____

Did You Know?
Are You Invisible on Facebook?

In 2013, Facebook admitted that the average post was visible to only 16 percent of those who liked the page. Research by the well-known ad agency Ogilvy & Mather found that number closer to 6 percent. Most recently, in 2015, research showed it may be as low as 2.6%. Organic posting without ads is not enough. Fan marketing is broken.

Insider Tip
Reaching Up

As discussed throughout this chapter, Facebook Messenger isn't great for supporting your team. However, Messenger is a wonderful way to stay in touch with a select group of distributors, such as those you personally sponsor or those you consider leaders. You may want to share private information with these people that you do not share with your entire team.

Facebook Messenger is becoming more like text. It's a way to communicate quickly, and your phone notifies you with new messages.

Facebook Pages is an excellent way to grow your business if you are willing to spend money on Facebook Advertising to find new prospects and stay in touch with those who like your page. Since money is involved to grow a successful page, most distributors should focus on their profile until they start to earn money from being a distributor. At that point, it might make sense to revisit a Facebook Page.

Mental Check
Limitations

You've been using Facebook Messenger to chat with your distributors, and you might have a Facebook Page for your business. Think of the following.

Facebook Messenger is messy when many people are part of the conversation. Think about receiving a message with 100 other people attached to it. By the time you opened up the message, 80 others already read it. Everyone is giving thumbs up and commenting. You cannot read the original message without scrolling to the top. Many recipients don't realize they should scroll to the top, so they miss valuable information.

Outside of the network marketing profession, Facebook Pages have served business owners and entrepreneurs well. These types of businesses have the resources, capital, and people to build successful Facebook Pages. We aren't saying Facebook Pages should never be used for your business.

Everything has a time and place. There is a new breed of entrepreneurs called solopreneurs. These are entrepreneurs with no employees. A network marketing distributor would be a solopreneur. A solopreneur is selling a product or service from their home to friends, family and referrals.

This is best done through your personal profile as long as you are a professional.

	Exercise	
	Obstacles	

Let's make sure you believe Facebook Messenger and Facebook Pages aren't good enough.

Today, try using Facebook Messenger to support your distributors. What three obstacles do you encounter?

1. _____

2. _____

3. _____

Today, try using Facebook Pages to support your distributors. What three obstacles do you encounter?

1. _____

2. _____

3. _____

By completing these exercises, you'll find Facebook Messenger and Facebook Pages don't work as well as Facebook Group for network marketing purposes. Support is crucial. Using the right support tool makes all the difference in how your distributors perform long term in the network marketing profession.

Facebook Group is More Effective Than Facebook Messenger and a Facebook Business Page

	Knowledge Check 3.3	
	(Circle your answer)	

T	F	Facebook Groups are a set of private online communities.
T	F	You can invite a friend interested in your business to a Facebook Group; however, it won't motivate your friend to enroll sooner as a customer or distributor.
		When you post or comment in a Facebook Group, everyone is notified. This notification shows up in which icon?
	a.	World Icon
	b.	Message Icon
	c.	People Icon
	d.	None of the Above
	e.	All of the Above

		For which of the following should you use Facebook Group?
	a.	Ask questions
	b.	Seek advice
	c.	Share product testimonials and success tips
	d.	Organize events
	e.	All of the Above

Fill In The Blank
Team Support with Facebook Groups

Do you currently use a Facebook Group to support your team? What do you like most about the group?

_____

_____

_____

_____

_____

_____

Did You Know?
Where Conversation is King

Compared to any other outlet found on Facebook, Facebook Groups is where real conversations (engagement) happen around your product and opportunity.

Insider Tip
Facebook Group Engagement Results

Your company may have a Facebook Group. A distributor above you, who earns a full-time income, may have a group, as well. Choose the group that works the best for you.

In December 2012, I ran a test to see what happened if I implemented and ran a Facebook Group properly during one of the slowest times of the year for the network marketing profession. The results were amazing:

- 40 distributors from the company joined the group
- 230 prospects, referred by the 40 distributors, joined the group
- 23 prospects enrolled as a distributor.
- The Facebook Group generated over $24,000 in product sales

Insider Tip (continued)
Facebook Group Engagement Results

Notice that one out of 10 prospects became a distributor. The profession, as a whole, experiences one out of 20. Facebook Groups have the potential to make our profession better.

Mental Check
Think About It

Distributors are trained to promote the next event. If distributors attend an event, the chances of a successful event increase exponentially.

This occurs because distributors network with each other, building a strong culture. Distributors are trained directly from the most successful distributors in the company. A Facebook Group that is run properly achieves the same outcome every day, seven days a week. Get your distributors to the next event. More importantly, run a successful Facebook Group for your distributors.

Exercise
Passion-Based Facebook Groups

Let's make sure you believe Facebook Group is more effective than Facebook Messenger and a Facebook Business Page.

Join a Facebook Group based on a topic you love, like horseback riding or cooking. Interact with the other members. Answer the following questions:

- Was it easy to join the group? _____

- Was it easy to speak with others? _____

- Was it easy to share stories on the topic you love? _____

- Rate your overall experience: 1   2   3   4   5   6   7   8   9   10

By completing this exercise, you'll understand how Facebook Group can support you and your distributors. Making support easy allows your distributors faster success.

How Facebook Groups Create Social Proof – And Sales!

Fill In The Blank
Write It Down

In your own words, what is social proof? How has it affected your business so far?

_____

_____

_____

_____

Did You Know?
Knowledge Check

There are five types of social proof – expert, celebrity, user, wisdom of the crowds, and your friends.

Insider Tip
Social Proof

The best way to create social proof in a Facebook Group is to start with you. Consistently enroll new customers and distributors, and add them to the Facebook Group as well as prospects. When others see you produce, they'll want to produce, too.

The worst that can happen is that you fall into management mode, overseeing other distributors' productivity and not producing yourself.

Mark Yarnell taught me to never stop enrolling distributors and customers myself. As a result of this practice:

- When I focused on personal production, my team was inspired by my production and wanted to be successful, too. The team continued to enroll new distributors and customers. Each distributor knew success was within their grasp because they saw me succeed.

- When I focused on supporting my team and not personally producing, my team slowly stopped building. When I tried to encourage my team to keep going, distributors gave me many excuses on why they couldn't enroll a new distributor or customer. Team member excuses ranged from something wrong with the website to the conviction that no one in their area was interested to the belief that weren't good enough.

As wonderful as social proof is for your business, it can hurt your business. For example, members in your group may become upset because one of the company products is not available for sale anymore. A distributor might post her frustration to the group. Another 10 distributors might join in on the frustration causing an inappropriate scene.

Teach your distributors to be positive in the group. If something negative surfaces, ask your distributor to contact you privately. If someone posts a negative message in the group, address it publicly first. If this is not possible, delete the post and contact the member privately to address it. This is your group, so protect it.

Mental Check
It Can Go Either Way

Social Proof can cause havoc or momentum for your team.

Havoc occurs when you do not lead the group like you would lead your team at live events and on phone calls. You let negativity breed in the group, which turns into conflict. Worse, distributors leave your company, pulling other distributors with them to a new network marketing company.

Momentum occurs when the opposite happens. You squash negativity before it has an opportunity to perpetuate. You keep the group moving in a positive direction by personally producing at all times, no matter your income.

Social proof is a powerful thing.

Let's make sure you understand social proof.

Write three ideas to create social proof. For each of the next three weeks, implement one of the suggestions.

1. _____

2. _____

3. _____

Today, practice being observant. Social proof is happening all around us. Whether it is face to face or on Facebook, watch for groups of people gathering together then find out why. For example, a musician is performing on the corner. A group forms to watch, so others walking by slow down. No doubt, they suspect the musician must be good because she generated a crowd(social proof). A picture of a crowd forming outside a local Walmart appears as a Facebook post in your Newsfeed. People might think a sale is going on and head to Walmart to take advantage of it (social proof). Write three times in your life when you believe social proof happened.

1. _____

2. _____

3. _____

By completing these exercises, you'll gain a better understanding of how social proof affects us and our business on a daily basis. Social Proof can be good and bad. Make it good for your business by harnessing the power of others.

How Distributors Can Get The Most Out Of Facebook Groups

		Knowledge Check 3.5
		(Circle your answer)
T	F	Visit the group several times a week. The time of day doesn't matter.
T	F	Comment on every Facebook post in the group.
T	F	Post something in the group at least once every two weeks.

77

Knowledge Check 3.5 (continued)
(Circle your answer)

		What type of Facebook posts aren't appropriate to post?
	a.	Questions
	b.	Words of motivation
	c.	Personal post, not business related, about your life
	d.	None of the Above
	e.	All of the Above

Fill In The Blank
It's a Numbers Game

How many prospects did you add to your company's Facebook group over the past 30 days?

_____

If you're not happy with how fast your business is growing, add more prospects to the group. In our research, we've found that one out of every 10 people who were invited to a group enrolled as a consultant within 60 days.

Did You Know?
You Can Do It

It takes just 10 minutes a day to participate in your company's Facebook Group.

Insider Tip
The Law of Reciprocation

The law of reciprocation is based on give and take. If you do something for someone, he will do something for you. In a Facebook group, distributors invite their prospects into the group. Comment on other distributors' posts so they comment on your posts when you invite your friends.

Here is a cheat sheet:

- Scroll through the group newsfeed and like or comment on everyone's posts.

- Next, write your own post. Ask a question or share some motivation or business updates. Examples of business updates:
    - I signed up 1 new customer today and 2 distributors!
    - I sent out 4 samples! This is exciting!
    - I spoke to 8 new people today about my business.
    - I would like for you to meet my friend, Alexa Harrington. She is interested in the business...

The level of activity in a Facebook Group can seem overwhelming at times. Try to have fun with it. Take baby steps. Facebook Group will be one of the strongest pieces to your success.

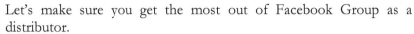

Exercise
How to Win with Facebook Groups

Let's make sure you get the most out of Facebook Group as a distributor.

Set a daily reminder and include the message below with the reminder in your cell phone.

I, _____, make a commitment to spend 10 minutes a day, Monday-Friday, in my business Facebook Group.

Life is fun when you work and play with others. Choose one person in your Facebook Group whom you see as a friend outside of business. Make an agreement with that person to hold each other accountable. It's interesting how fast we succeed when we know others are watching us. Who did you choose?

_____

Be an action taker, not an observer. Many people like to observe the Facebook group, learn from everyone else, and remain quiet. Make it a goal to interact in the group by asking a question or sharing words of motivation and what you did this week in your business.

By completing these exercises, you'll start to use Facebook Group properly as a distributor. Once you use it consistently and effectively, you'll experience the benefits of a Facebook Group.

How Admins Can Get The Most Out Of Facebook Groups

		Knowledge Check 3.6
		(Circle your answer)
T	F	As an admin of the group, check into the group at least every other day.
T	F	It's your responsibility to lead the group. The success or failure of the group is dependent on your leadership.
T	F	Interact with others the same way members do.
T	F	It's good to get approval from your company before using the company name in the Facebook group name.

Knowledge Check 3.6
(Circle your answer)

Which of the following should you be doing in the Facebook group?

a. Answering questions
b. Giving words of motivation
c. Welcoming new people to the group by leaving a comment
d. None of the Above
e. All of the Above

How many times should you post something in the group per week?

a. 1
b. 7
c. 3
d. 14
e. None of the Above

Fill In The Blank
Think Ahead

If you enrolled us as a distributor in your business today, what would you teach us over the next 30 days to help us be successful distributors?

_____

_____

_____

_____

_____

Did You Know?
It's Easy

It takes just 20 minutes a day to be a successful admin of your Facebook Group.

Insider Tip
The Law of Reciprocation

How important is it to be a strong admin of the group? As I mentioned throughout the book and workbook, it's crucial.

Insider Tip (continued)
The Law of Reciprocation

In 2013, a woman reached out to me on Facebook Messenger. She was frustrated with her business because it wasn't growing as fast as she would like. I asked her if she was part of the group where I was an admin. She said no, and I asked her to become a member.

After a year of my support, she earned the second highest rank in the company's compensation plan.

With just a little help, anyone can go a long way in the network marketing profession.

Mental Check
It's Okay to Team Up

Being a Facebook group admin is a great responsibility. If you don't feel ready, it's good to have a co-admin or several admins. If you aren't an admin of a group yet, don't worry. Your time will come. You're developing into a leader.

Other distributors look to you for guidance. Let's say you have a team of 5,000 distributors. What if you did a motivational post today? And what if the instant you published it, all 5000 distributors had the opportunity to be inspired by you? What would that do for their business activity? Inspire someone today.

Exercise
Lead & Teach Through Posts

Let's make sure you get the most out of Facebook Group as an admin.

In the 'fill in the blank' section above, you shared what you would teach us if we were distributors. Turn three of your teachings into Facebook posts and share them in the Facebook Group over the next week. What are your three posts?

Post One:	
Post Two:	
Post Three:	

Click on notifications at the top of your Facebook Group and choose all posts today. All posts should be checkmarked to ensure you are notified every time someone posts, likes and comments in the group. If the notifications become overwhelming, you can turn the notifications off and visit the group to see new notifications.

Did you complete this task? (circle your answer)   Yes   No

Go to edit group settings and complete the following today:

Membership Approval: Please select "Any member can add members", but an admin must approve them.

Did you complete this task? (circle your answer)   Yes   No

Description: Write a short paragraph that explains your business. Potential members see the description if privacy is set to open or closed. The description is a good place to put a few sentences on group policy. What is allowed and what isn't? Later, if you see any behavior you don't like, modify this description to address it.

Did you complete this task? (circle your answer)   Yes   No

Tags: Insert words related to your product and business today. Tags help people find groups about certain topics. This can help generate new leads for you and your team.

Did you complete this task? (circle your answer)   Yes   No

Posting Permissions: Allow members and admins to post to the group, because everyone actively engaging in the group is crucial for the group success.

Did you complete this task? (circle your answer)   Yes   No

Post Approval: We suggest you approve all group posts before other group members see the posts. This protects you from someone spamming your group.

Did you complete this task? (circle your answer)   Yes   No

Using the event feature, create three events—one local, one regional, and one national. More people will show up at your events when you utilize this feature on Facebook.

	Event Name	When	Where
1.	_____	_____	_____
2.	_____	_____	_____
3.	_____	_____	_____

It's time to write your pinned post. A good pin post sets the tone of the group. It tells members the purpose of the group and how they should act. In a few short sentences, write it below.

_____

_____

_____

_____

_____

Most successful distributors create unique training based on their individual style. Create one new document or upload a file to share your training with your team today. Members can edit these documents, so you might want to create the documents as a PDF to protect your materials from being altered by others.

Did you complete this task? (circle your answer)   Yes   No

By completing these exercises, you'll start to use the Facebook Group properly as an admin. Remember, the success of a Facebook Group is your responsibility.

When and How To Add Friends To A Facebook Group

T	F	Add a friend if you think she would be great as a distributor in your business.
T	F	It's okay to add your friends to the group without their consent.

Fill In The Blank
Get 'Er Done

How many friends have you invited to your Facebook group in the last 30 days?

_____

Did You Know?
A Preview of Coming Attractions

The small act of adding your friends to a Facebook Group increases the chances of your friends becoming distributors because it gives them a sneak peek into the culture of your company.

Insider Tip
Making Introductions

When adding a friend who is interested in the business to your group, it's important you introduce your friend properly. You want to be as detailed as possible so others might be able to share a story that motivates your friend to enroll as a distributor.

Here are two examples:

1. Example One: "I would like to introduce you to my friend, Alexa Harrington. She is interested in learning more about the business. She tried a sample of our product and loves how it makes her skin soft. Her daughter has acne, so she hopes the product will help her. She is thinking about the business because she would like to make some extra money to take her family on more vacations. Please share with her why you like our business."

2. Example Two: "I would like to introduce you to my friend, Alexa Harrington. Please tell her why you love our business!"

Example one allows another distributor to comment and say, "Hey Alexa! I've been in the business for two years and now make enough money to take my family on two vacations a year. This is a wonderful business! By the way, my family and I just got back from Disney."

Inviting this type of response is sure to motivate your friend.

Mental Check
Create a Winning Culture

When you add a prospect to the group, you may be nervous your prospect will enroll as a distributor with someone else in the group because you're not yet successful. When a leader builds the right environment in the group, this is never an issue. Remember, teamwork makes the dream work.

Also, some of us have an ego. We think we can do the work ourselves. We don't believe we need the assistance of others to inspire someone to enroll as a distributor. Put your ego aside and embrace social proof. Start adding people to the group today.

Exercise
Introducing...

Let's make sure you know how to introduce your friends and respond to others who are introducing their friends to the Facebook Group.

Your friend, Patricia, has an interest in becoming a distributor for your company. You met her eight years ago in a yoga class and became like sisters. She is interested in the business because she is stressed at work, can't find enough money to pay the bills, and wishes she had more time with her two-year-old daughter.

In your own words, how would you introduce Patricia to the group? Remember to welcome her, say something personal about your relationship, and finish by telling the group why she is thinking about becoming a distributor.

_____

_____

_____

_____

When someone else in the group adds a friend, welcome her by leaving a comment. For example, "Hi Marianne! Welcome to the group! I joined this business because the product helped me personally. I lost 15 pounds and kept it off! I also wanted to earn a part-time income from home, so I had more money to go on vacations with my family. So far, I have three customers, and I'm just getting started!" You will inspire this new person, and others will comment when you add your friends.

Share your personal story today. Be detailed so it's group-ready. Always customize it based on why the person is interested in becoming a distributor.

_____

_____

_____

_____

By completing these exercises, you'll become better at communicating in the Facebook Group. Using the right words inspires others to take action.

Final Thoughts

A network marketing professional promotes the next event because an event inspires and motivates a distributor. An event can be a phone call, video chat, webinar, party, or a local, regional or national event.

A Facebook Group is like an event, but it's happening 24 hours a day. When run correctly, a Facebook Group becomes the cornerstone of your Facebook success. Give inspiration to your team and motivate your distributor-prospects to be their very best.

What are your five biggest takeaways from this chapter?

1. _____

2. _____

3. _____

4. _____

5. _____

NOTES:

_____

_____

_____

_____

_____

_____

_____

_____

_____

_____

_____

_____

_____

_____

_____

_____

_____

_____

_____

_____

_____

_____

_____

Chapter 4

What Your Facebook Profile Says About You

C an you imagine a place online where a potential customer could learn a great deal about you through text, pictures, and videos before she speaks with you on the phone or meets face to face?

Not only would this be cool, but it would allow you to help this person become a customer or distributor much faster since she would already know, like, and trust you.

Let's learn how a Facebook Profile grows your business!

Take a moment to refresh your knowledge of chapter five in *Network Marketing For Facebook*. Then complete this workbook section.

		Knowledge Check 4.1 (Circle your answer)
T	F	Your Profile Picture, Cover Image, and "About" section are the most important pieces of your profile for your network marketing business.
T	F	If you have an excellent product, others don't need to know, like, and trust you before sampling your product.
T	F	Your profile is a way to organize your life and tell your story on Facebook.

Fill In The Blank
Your Favorite Things

What three features do you like the most on your Facebook Profile?

1. _____

2. _____

3. _____

Did You Know?
For Real

Out of 81 million Facebook Profiles, only about 5% are fake

Insider Tip
Be Yourself

A few years ago, I learned the following.

- 25 percent of people will never like you, no matter what you do.

- 25 percent of people will not like you at first but may be persuaded to change their opinion of you.

- 25 percent of people will like you at first but may be persuaded to change their opinion of you.

- 25 percent of people will like you no matter what.

Be yourself when growing your profile. Seventy-five percent of people you meet can be your friend.

Mental Check
Control Your Privacy or Openness

Facebook allows you to adjust your privacy settings so everyone, friends, friends of friends, or certain people can or cannot see your profile.

You have complete control over your life on Facebook.

Exercise
Who Are You?

Let's make sure you create the right Facebook Profile.

Take some time alone today. Reflect on who you are, what you stand for, and what you believe in. It's important to have a sense of self, in life and in business. When you're comfortable being who you are, that confidence reflects in your profile.

Remember, 25% of people will never like you, no matter what you do. You can't please everyone. Focus on being who you want to be as you create your FB profile.

Answer the three questions below.

1. Who are you?	

2. What do you stand for?	
3. What do you believe in?	

By completing this exercise, you'll gain a better understanding of who you are as a person. By understanding you, the right person can shine brightly through your Facebook Profile. You will lift others and show there is a better way to live, whether it is through using your products or being successful as a distributor in your company.

Step 1: Getting to Know You

Knowledge Check 4.2
(Circle your answer)

T	F	People will come to trust you by your Profile Picture.
T	F	You should be the only person in your profile picture.
		Which of the following are important for your profile picture?
	a.	A close-up shot of you with a bright smile
	b.	A professional image
	c.	A photo that incorporates your personality
	d.	None of the above
	e.	All of the above
		Which of the following are acceptable to include in your profile picture?
	a.	You holding your product
	b.	Your significant other
	c.	Your children
	d.	Your pets
	e.	None of the Above

Fill In The Blank
Changes...

How many times in the last year have you changed your profile picture?

_____

Did You Know?
Kinda Like Your Real-Life Face

By default, your profile picture is public.

Insider Tip
Don't Change
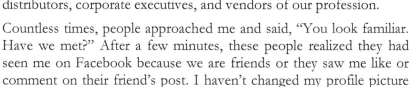

I attended a network marketing event in Las Vegas with 8,000 distributors, corporate executives, and vendors of our profession.

Countless times, people approached me and said, "You look familiar. Have we met?" After a few minutes, these people realized they had seen me on Facebook because we are friends or they saw me like or comment on their friend's post. I haven't changed my profile picture in years because I know people who see my face over and over again will recognize me in public and say hello.

The most successful brands in the world, like Nike, Apple, Facebook and Starbucks, rarely change their logo. A company's logo is the equivalent of your profile picture. Shouldn't we emulate their success?

Mental Check
Be You

Some people are self-conscious about their smile or teeth. Smile anyway. Nobody's perfect! When people look at your profile picture, they just want to know you're friendly. Smile away!

Exercise
Good & Bad Profile Pictures

The newsfeed is a collection of your friends' posts that you see as soon as you log into Facebook. Next to each post is a small picture identifying the person who wrote the post. This is your profile picture. Look in your newsfeed today. Whose five profile pictures can you see clearly? Whose are difficult to see?

	Clear	Difficult to See
1.	_____	_____
2.	_____	_____
3.	_____	_____
4.	_____	_____
5.	_____	_____

Out of the profile pictures above, note why each picture is clear or difficult to see.

	Clear (why)	Difficult to See (why)
1.	_____	_____
2.	_____	_____
3.	_____	_____
4.	_____	_____
5.	_____	_____

Are you having difficulty finding the perfect profile picture? Consider having a professional headshot taken by a local photographer. The cost is minimal and the experience will last a lifetime. Schedule a time to get your picture done professionally.

Date scheduled: _____

By completing these exercises, you'll find your best Profile picture. Your Profile picture is the doorway to your profile and your first impression on Facebook.

Step 2: Beginning to Like You

T	F	People will come to know you by your cover image.
T	F	Your cover image is a way for others to get a glimpse into your life.
T	F	It's impossible to turn others off when posting a cover image because you're just sharing your life.

		Which of the following images are great to use as a cover image?
	a.	You receiving an award for your accomplishments in network marketing
	b.	You hiking the mountains on a nearby trail
	c.	Your family enjoying a holiday dinner
	d.	Drinking Mai Tai's on your last trip to Cozumel
	e.	All of the above
		Which of the following statement(s) are true?
	a.	The cover image is not another way to build relationships
	b.	Constantly change your cover image to keep current with what's going on in your life
	c.	Don't post images on topics that are controversial unless you want to lose business
	d.	All of the above
	e.	b and c

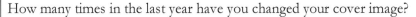

Fill In The Blank
Changes…

How many times in the last year have you changed your cover image?

_____

Did You Know?
It's Your Theme

The cover image was introduced by Facebook in 2011.

Insider Tip
Your Cover Image Matters

One of my coaching clients, Alicia, recently updated her cover image. As a result, a friend liked the post that notified Alicia's friends of her new cover image. Alicia thanked her friend, and a conversation started about the product. Alicia's friend tried the product, became a customer, and lost 13 pounds. Alicia's friend is now referring people to her. This successful chain of events began when Alicia updated her cover image.

On the other hand, I've seen distributors who never change their cover image or only use a company logo for the cover. I can guarantee you these distributors have never received a new distributor or customer from their cover image.

Mental Check
Let People Get To Know You & Your Life

Some people are anxious about showing pictures of their children, loved ones, and life events. When you set up your profile correctly and are professional with your business, you'll attract people who would be your friend in real life. Most people are not anxious about sharing aspects of their life with real friends.

Remember, the purpose of your cover image is to help others develop an authentic impression of you.

Exercise
Cover Images

Visit five of your friends' Facebook Profiles today. Write down each friend's name and the primary emotion you felt while looking at the cover images.

Friend's Name	Emotion You Felt
1.	
2.	
3.	
4.	
5.	

Ask five Facebook friends to give an opinion of your cover image. You're looking for emotional responses. For example, your cover image may be a photo of you receiving an award at your network marketing national convention. Your friend may say, "It looks like you are having a lot of fun and are doing well." Write feedback on the lines below.

Friend's Name	Opinion
1.	
2.	
3.	
4.	
5.	

Exercise (continued)
Cover Images

Choose five pictures that put a smile on your face. Use these pictures as future cover images. Which five pictures did you choose?

1. _____
2. _____
3. _____
4. _____
5. _____

By completing these exercises, you'll use cover images that provoke emotion on your Facebook Profile. Your cover image is like a title of a book. If you catch someone's interest, he will explore your profile.

Step 3: Beginning to Trust You

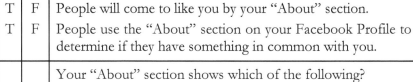

Knowledge Check 4.4
(Circle your answer)

| T | F | People will come to like you by your "About" section. |
| T | F | People use the "About" section on your Facebook Profile to determine if they have something in common with you. |

	Your "About" section shows which of the following?
a.	Work history, education, where you went to high school and college
b.	Where you currently live and have lived, contact, and basic information
c.	Favorite books, music, movies, and TV shows
d.	None of the above
e.	All of the above

Fill In The Blank
Fill It Out

Is your "About" section filled out as detailed as www.facebook.com/jimlupkin?

_____

Did You Know?
You're Closer to Kevin Bacon Than You Think

There are, on average, 3.74 degrees of separation between any one Facebook user and another. It's easy to find people on Facebook as long as you have commonalities to build trust.

Insider Tip
About You

As you use Graph Search to increase your Facebook friends, most of these people will check out your "About" section to see if they like who you are before accepting your friend request. Those who have a detailed "About" section will capture a lot more new friends than those who don't fill it out.

Another way to use the "About" section is right before you jump on the phone or a Facebook Video Chat with someone. You might say, "Hey Mary! Before we jump on the phone to discuss my business, please check out my "About" section so you can learn more about me. Here is the link (insert link). I will also look at your "About" section so I can learn more about you. Looking forward to our call!"

By looking at each other's "About" section prior to a call, you'll notice your friend will move ahead as a customer or distributor in a shorter period of time.

I went from making sixty-minute phone calls to twenty-minute calls. I learned that 20 minutes delivers the same results, as long as I had familiarity with the person on the other end of the line prior to the call. To put it another way, it used to take me 40 hours a week to enroll 30 new distributors a month. Having a detailed "About" section online reduced this number to 20 hours a week. My college professor taught me that the only even playing field in business is time. Those who use their time more effectively win every time.

Mental Check
The Truth Is Powerful

You may believe your "About" section is too personal. Maybe you're not proud about your past. Remember, it's not where you came from but where you are going that counts. Living in a bad neighborhood or working a minimum wage job will show people how far you have come. Be proud who you are. This inspires people. Many people are facing similar struggles.

Let's make sure step three makes sense to you.

Visit five of your friend's Facebook Profiles today. Write each friends name and what you learned about each friend when reading your friend's "About" section.

	Friend's Name	What You Learned
1.		
2.		
3.		
4.		
5.		

Ask five Facebook friends to read your "About" section. List something each friend learned about you.

	Friend's Name	What You Learned
1.		
2.		
3.		
4.		
5.		

Go to www.facebook.com/jimlupkin/about and write what you liked about each piece of Jim's "About" section.

What did you like about Jim's work and education?	
What did you like about Jim's places he lived?	
What did you like about Jim's contact and basic info?	
What did you like about Jim's family and relationships?	

Exercise (continued)
Profile Impact
What did you like about Jim's details about him?
What did you like about Jim's life events?

By completing these exercises, you'll realize the more detailed you are with your "About" section, the more successful you'll be as a distributor. The more open you are, the more people can get to know, like, and trust you.

Work History

Knowledge Check 4.5		
(Circle your answer)		
T	F	Include your entire work history, even if it dates back 20 years

Fill In The Blank
Truth
How many jobs have you had in your lifetime?

Did You Know?
No Way!
Most people have had more than six jobs by the time they're 25 years old.

Insider Tip
Your History Opens Doors & Hearts
By sharing your work history, you'll connect to others who have worked or still work at those same companies. Commonality helps build relationships.
In 2009, I was a distributor for a network marketing company. I remember speaking with Tom about my company.

Tom: "I noticed you were in ACN back in the 90s."

Me: "Yes! It was a wonderful experience. It was my first exposure to network marketing."

Tom: "Did you know a guy by the name of Orin S?"

Me: "Oh, yes! He was in my sponsor. I really liked him."

Tom: "I really liked him, too. Small world, huh?"

Me: "Sure is. I'm glad we met."

Tom: "Me too. Tell me about your business. I'm all ears."

Knowing my work history made a difference in how Tom looked at my company.

Mental Check
If He/She Can Do It, Maybe I Can Too

Some of us are embarrassed by certain jobs because of how society views those jobs. Don't be ashamed if your career is not stellar. Telling everyone you are the VP of Marketing for XYZ Company will not grow your business. Being honest and transparent about your work history builds relationships, and relationships grow your business. Often people find it easier to connect to someone who comes from less-than-stellar origins, or who is at the same experience level.

Exercise
Memory Lane

Let's make sure you complete your work history.

Filling out your entire work history can feel daunting. Make it a fun activity to go down memory lane. Every job you write down opens the door to more potential prospects. Write the name of each employer, the years you were employed, your job title, and the job description for your last five jobs.

	Employer	Years	Job Title	Job Description
1.				
2.				
3.				
4.				
5.				

Exercise (continued)
Memory Lane

Take a moment and reflect on your past employment by answering these questions.

Which three friends did you enjoy working with out of all your jobs?

1. _____

2. _____

3. _____

Who were your favorite three bosses?

1. _____

2. _____

3. _____

By completing this exercise, you'll have an understanding of the details needed for your work history. The more detailed you are, the more your commonalities can help you connect with people about your business.

High School and College

Knowledge Check 4.6
(Circle your answer)

T	F	Include your high school and college information because it will help connect you with others who attended the same schools.

Fill In The Blank
Old School

In your own words, how would you describe your high school and college experiences?

_____

_____

_____

_____

_____

Did You Know?
High School's Cool

The average high school in the U.S. has more than 800 students at any given time. In your business, this translates to 800 possible customers and distributors!

Insider Tip
Creating Common Ground

Often, attending the same school is enough to create trust with an otherwise complete stranger.

Because of Facebook, I've been able to stay in touch with college friends from around the world. This allows me to quickly network in more than a dozen different countries at any given time.

Many distributors don't realize you don't have to be college friends or have been in school at the same time to reach out to those who attended your college.

My graduating class was 2004. I could reach out to any of the students who graduated with me because we both graduated the same year. We have something in common.

I could also reach out to those who graduated three years before or three years after me and still have something in common. We both attended the same school at the same time.

Years ago, I became friends with an older gentleman who graduated from my college more than twenty years before I attended. We still had fun talking about how much the school had evolved in that time. Common ground creates easy conversations, which turn into relationships and future customers and distributors.

What I just shared with you holds true for high school, as well.

Mental Check
Old Baggage

Were you popular in high school? Maybe not, and it's holding you back from connecting with your old classmates. But think about it- most people weren't popular. Only the popular kids were! And the reality is that you're no longer the same person you were in high school. Chances are, neither are your classmates. In fact, they've probably changed more than you think. And you never know who is looking for an opportunity.

Let's make sure you complete your high school and college information.

Filling out your high school and college information might sound simple. However, it's easy to miss the little things that makes this part powerful. Write the name of your schools, years attended, major, and description of what you accomplished in each school.

	School Name	Years	Major	Description
1.	_____	_____	_____	_____
2.	_____	_____	_____	_____
3.	_____	_____	_____	_____
4.	_____	_____	_____	_____
5.	_____	_____	_____	_____

Take a moment and reflect on the good old days by answering these questions.

Which three friends did you hang out with?
1. _____
2. _____
3. _____

Which three friends did you believe were going to do something great with their lives?
1. _____
2. _____
3. _____

Which three names popped in your head when you said, "I wonder where they are now?"
1. _____
2. _____
3. _____

By completing this exercise, you'll fill out your school information correctly. Reach out to a few people via Facebook, and you'll be setting yourself up for thousands of potential contacts. Learning how to access high school and college contacts opens you up to more than enough people to speak with for the rest of your network marketing career.

Where You're Living, Have Lived and Hometown:

		Knowledge Check 4.7 (Circle your answer)
T	F	Where you're currently living will connect you to more people than where you've lived and your hometown.

Fill In The Blank
Hometowns

List the places in which you have lived, beginning with your hometown. Write a one-sentence description of each place. What key words did you use that might create a sense of commonality with potential customers?

_____

_____

_____

_____

Did You Know?
Movin' On Up

People move, on average, more than 11 times in their lifetime. This equates to 11 opportunities to find new circles of friends with whom to share your product and business.

Insider Tip
Sharing your Info

By sharing where you're living, where you have lived, and your hometown, you'll connect with others who are from the same areas. Your hometown, alone, represents thousands of potential customers and distributors for your business. Just like your school, common geography builds trust with an otherwise complete stranger.

About four years ago, one of my coaching students, Marianne, connected with an old friend from her hometown because they both listed the same town in their "About" section.

After a few months of being friends on Facebook, her friend did a post asking if anyone knew of job opportunities. His town had a population of 7,000 people. Jobs were scarce and the lack of opportunity created a negative vibe amongst everyone in town. Marianne introduced him to the network marketing profession. Within a year, he had a team of 20 distributors, growing in what many would consider an impossible place to grow a business.

Insider Tip (continued)
Sharing your Info

Everyone everywhere is looking for opportunity. Be the person to introduce your friends to the network marketing profession. When you list where you live, have lived, and hometown, you open your business up to hundreds of thousands of people, if not millions. The possibilities are endless.

Mental Check
Detroit, New York City & Peoria

Does your town have a depressed economy and you think locals are not open to opportunities? Is your city large and you believe people are focused on their big-time careers?

People are people. We all want a better life for our loved ones. In today's world, we all know job security can be fleeting. Feel confident that you are giving people a new and viable option that could be a great opportunity for them and their families.

Exercise
I Get Around

Filling out your current city, have lived, and hometown opens you up to a tremendous amount of potential customers and distributors for your business.

Places I have lived	Years
1. _____	_____
2. _____	_____
3. _____	_____
4. _____	_____
5. _____	_____

Sometimes we forget whom we've met in our life. Take a moment and really think about each place you lived by answering the following questions.

Which three neighbors were your favorites?

1. _____

2. _____

3. _____

Which three people in your community did you enjoy visiting, like the mailman or owner of the bakery down the street from your home?

1. _____

2. _____

3. _____

Which three parents did you resonate with when your kids hung out with their kids?

1. _____

2. _____

3. _____

By completing these exercises, you'll remember the places you lived and appreciate how this part of Facebook can open you up to many new possible customers and distributors. Learning how to access people who live in your current city, hometown, or places you have lived introduces you to hundreds of thousands of people who might be looking for your type of product or an opportunity to make extra money as a distributor.

Contact and Basic Information

Knowledge Check 4.8
(Circle your answer)

T	F	Make all of your information available in this section, including your address.

Fill In The Blank
Here, Take My Card

In the past 30 days, how many times have you given out your contact information when discussing your business face to face?

_____

Did You Know?
Are You On Facebook?

More and more people are using Facebook as a digital address book.

You don't have to share your contact information with everyone on Facebook. You can choose to make it visible to 'only friends.'

By sharing your contact and basic information, you'll allow others to connect with you and build relationships faster. As an example, one feature in basic information is your birthdate. Two people wishing each other "happy birthday" are building their relationship.

Mental Check
An E-Business Card

Are you nervous about putting your phone number and email address in your "About" section? Your profile is your business card. Wouldn't you put this information on a business card? How is this different? It's not. You want people to have access to you.

Exercise
Profile Basics

Let's make sure you complete your contact and basic information.

Answer the following questions to help you fill out this information effortlessly:

- What is your mobile phone number? _____
- What is your email address? _____
- What is your distributor website address? _____
- When were you born? _____
- What are your religious views? _____
- What are your political views? _____
- What languages can you speak? _____

By completing this exercise, you'll give others more information about you so you can build stronger relationships with your Facebook friends. Building relationships is easy on Facebook when using all of Facebook's available features.

Personal Relationships

Knowledge Check 4.9
(Circle your answer)

| T | F | By including these relationships, it gives you the opportunity to make new friends through people who already know, like, and trust you. |

Fill In The Blank
Stay Away, Aunt Marsha!

List three family members with whom you don't wish to connect on Facebook.

1. _____

2. _____

3. _____

Did You Know?
Facebook Is A Big Part of Our Culture

In 2011, one-third of all divorce filings in the US contained the word Facebook. More than 30 million deceased family members are still thought to still have a Facebook account.

Insider Tip
Don't Assume

My friend, Jeremy, has a cousin who doesn't believe network marketing is a good way to make a living. Because his cousin is closed-minded, Jeremy thinks all of his cousin's friends are the same.

One day, Jeremy saw his cousin's friend talk about network marketing in a Facebook post. Curious, Jeremy reached out to her through Facebook Messenger. Jeremy found out she recently joined the network marketing profession and is excited about what it can do for her life. Jeremy now kicks himself for not reaching out to her sooner.

Don't let this be you. Everyone is different.

You never know who might be looking for something to change their life. The power is the connection. The connection is a spouse or family member. This is a connection of trust. When you friend their friends, trust is already there and relationships grow faster.

Mental Check
Friends of Family

Are you embarrassed by your family members or just not that close to some of them? Remember, the average person is connected to 300 people through Facebook. If someone is a friend with your spouse or family member, it creates instant trust. Trust encourages people to look at your business.

It's possible that eccentric Aunt Linda might know a successful entrepreneur who is looking for the right business opportunity. That that opportunity could be your business.

Exercise
Family Friend Numbers

Let's make sure you explore your personal relationships.

Visit the profiles of your spouse, significant other, and family members. Check out how many friends each has on Facebook. These friends may be open to your product or opportunity if they know you are in a relationship or family member with their friend.

How many friends does each of the following have on Facebook?

Your spouse/significant other: _____   Your aunt: _____

Your mother: _____   Your uncle: _____

Your father: _____   Your cousins: _____

Your sister: _____   Your son: _____

Your brother: _____   Your daughter: _____

Next, add up the numbers above and place the answer below.

_____

By completing the exercise, you'll be motivated to fill out this area of your "About" section. You now have a better understanding of the potential customers and distributors waiting for you through those relationships you already have.

Favorite Books, Music, Movies and TV Shows:

Knowledge Check 4.10
(Circle your answer)

T	F	Trust increases with others when you share interests such as books, music, movies, and TV shows.

Fill In The Blank
House of Thrones, Game of Cards

What are your favorite TV shows?

_____   _____
_____   _____
_____   _____
_____   _____

Did You Know?
Spoiler Alert

69% of people have binged-watched TV shows. In 2014, 352 original scripted TV series aired. In 2015, HBO purchased 200 pilot episodes.

Insider Tip
Birds of a Feather

Many times throughout my career, I was able to create a conversation around a book, song, movie, or television show.

Before you connect with someone on the phone or Facebook Video Chat, see if you have anything in common with this person.

For example, you might have read the same book or movie. During the conversation you might say, "I saw you read the book _Influence_. What did you like most about it?" Maybe you watched the same movie. "I saw you watched the movie _Titanic_. Wasn't it sad at the end when …?"

You're creating the same type of conversations you have with your friends with whom you spend time outside of Facebook. These types of conversations build friendships, which turns into customers and distributors.

Mental Check
Oh Hey You Like...

If you visit a friend's profile and notice they've read the same books, listen to the same music, or watch the same movies or TV shows you have, that commonality is a great conversation starter. It might even lead to talk about your business.

Let's make sure you consider favorite books, music, movies, and TV shows.

Visit the Facebook Profile of 10 friends today. List one new thing you learned about each friend by paying attention to favorite books, music, movies, and TV shows.

	Facebook Friends	One New Thing You Learned About Your Friend
1.		
2.		
3.		
4.		
5.		
6.		
7.		
8.		
9.		
10.		

By completing the exercise, you'll be anxious to fill out this area of your "About" section. As you feel closer to these 10 friends now, so will others who read this portion of your "About" section.

Final Thoughts

Do you believe a Facebook Profile can grow your business?

You can get someone to know, like, and trust you through text, pictures, and videos before speaking with you on the phone or face to face.

A profile picture, cover image, and "About" section play a vital role in the success of your profile for your business.

Your profile creates opportunities for people to have something in common with you. Commonality between two people is the fastest way to build a strong relationship.

What are your five biggest takeaways from this chapter?

1. _____

2. _____

3. _____

4. _____

5. _____

NOTES:

Chapter 5

Go Public on Facebook

Doesn't it make sense to have a grand opening to your business on Facebook in the same way every store in your town had a grand opening?

Besides having fun with it, you're getting the word out quickly that you are in business and others should check it out.

Let's learn how a "Grand Launch" public post in the Newsfeed grows your business.

Take a few minutes now to reread or skim chapter six in *Network Marketing For Facebook* before completing this workbook section.

	Knowledge Check 5.1	
	(Circle your answer)	
	When is the best time to do a "Grand Launch" public post?	
a.	Anytime	
b.	Only weekends	
c.	Sunday – Thursday, between 8pm – 9pm in your time zone	
d.	All of the above	
e.	None of the above	

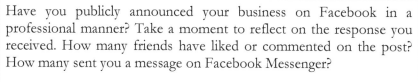

Fill In The Blank

Grand Reception

Have you publicly announced your business on Facebook in a professional manner? Take a moment to reflect on the response you received. How many friends have liked or commented on the post? How many sent you a message on Facebook Messenger?

_____

_____

_____

_____

Insider Tip
Announcements

Doing a "Grand Launch" public post is used almost daily by many distributors. I'm sure you would agree. You will achieve greater results if you do a "Grand Launch" public post only once per month.

Facebook was created to connect people, to build meaningful relationships. If you're advertising every day with this type of post, you're going against why Facebook exists. You might have already turned your Facebook friends off because you do this type of posting daily or weekly.

There are two easy ways to see if you are turning your friends off.

First, count the total number of posts you did over the last seven days. If more than 20% are business related then you're probably turning your friends off.

Second, look at commenters. Besides distributors in your company, is anyone else liking or commenting on your business posts? If not, you're probably turning your friends off.

I recommend you only do personal posts for the next 30 days before talking about business again if you are posting more than 20% business content or answered no to my last question. You need to reestablish relationships with your friends because, right now, your friends probably aren't listening. Worse, they might already be blocking you from their newsfeed, and you may not even know it.

Mental Check
Believe It

Why did you join the network marketing profession? Look at your why, believe in our profession, and know you can change the lives of those you care about through providing a remarkable product and opportunity to their lives. Share your business with your Facebook community in a professional manner by going public on Facebook.

Exercise		
Balance		

Review your Facebook posts. Mark a tally in one of the two columns below for each post in the past 30 days.

<u>Personal Posts</u>   <u>Business-related Posts</u>

_____   _____

Total both and reflect on your results. Are your friends getting to know you or is it mostly about business?

<u>Personal</u>   <u>Business-related</u>

_____   _____

By completing this exercise, you'll be able to know if you can do a "Grand Launch" public post immediately or take a few steps back and focus on building relationships with your friends because you posted too much about business in the last 30 days.

Three Easy Steps To Writing A Successful Post

		Knowledge Check 5.2
		(Circle your answer)
T	F	When writing a successful post, it's about closing your friend as a customer or consultant as fast as possible.
T	F	The following is an effective post: *I love my morning coffee! I found one that helps you lose weight. All you do is drink a cup a day and watch the pounds disappear. You can even keep eating the same way you do. I'll send you free samples!*
T	F	The following is an effective post: *Hey everyone! As you may know, I been trying to lose weight for years and nothing has helped. I recently lost 15 pounds and 11 inches. I'd love to show you how I did it. Please let me know if you'd like more information.*
T	F	The following is an effective post: *As you might know, I was recently diagnosed with Cancer. I started using this product and it cured me. I know that's a bold statement, but I would encourage you to check out the information first. Let me know.*

Knowledge Check 5.2 (continued)
(Circle your answer)

T	F	The following is an effective post: *I recently had a baby and needed ways to save money to offset baby expenses. My friend helped me save on my electricity bill. I saved almost $65 dollars last month. Would you like some information, as I am now promoting it to make extra money?*
T	F	The following is an effective post: *Unfortunately my grandmother gets sores on her body because she is bed ridden. She started using a new skincare cream and the sores disappeared overnight. I've been told these skincare products are curing skin conditions. We are excited! Would you like a sample?*
T	F	The following is an effective post: *Hey everyone! I have been hoping to take my son to Disney, but can't afford it. I found a travel company that has saved me 50%, so we are off to see Mickey Mouse this summer! I'm sharing this travel company with my friends as well.* *Would you like to check it out for your next vacation?*

Fill In The Blank
Announcing...

What were the words you used in your "Grand Launch" public post prior to reading our book?

_____

_____

Did You Know?
Everybody's Doing It

More than 500,000 new businesses are launched each month. Every one of these businesses goes public in their own way.

Insider Tip
3 Steps to Successful Posting

It takes only three easy steps to write a successful post.

Yes, it's *that* easy, yet many distributors make it difficult. Some distributors think they need to add something more because it's too simple.

Early in my network marketing career, I had the same opinion. I was a distributor for a very successful network marketing company. However, I had to create my own training materials because the company's training materials weren't good enough, in my mind. Of course, I was wrong. The time I spent developing my own materials could have been better spent on enrolling new customers and distributors.

While I was busy with my training materials, someone I knew enrolled as a distributor in this company with someone else. That contact could've been on my team had I not been busy doing something that wouldn't grow my business.

These three, simple steps work better than anything you can come up with. They've been tested over the past 20 years, with a 100,000 distributors producing over $100 million in sales with social media. Enjoy.

Mental Check
Tone It Down

Distributors often say things that are too good to be true, which limits a distributor's success. Limit the hype, and don't sound scammy. Be a professional, and watch your business soar by asking yourself this simple question: *"Would this post turn me off?"* Some of your most successful friends will join your business when you post in a professional manner.

Exercise
Do It

Let's make sure you understand the three easy steps to writing a successful post.

Step 1: Say, *"Hey everyone!"*

Step 2: Write one personal and one product statement. Insert yours here:

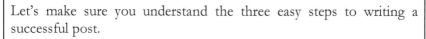

_____

_____

_____

Step 3: Add a question to continue the conversation. Insert yours here:

_____

_____

_____

Final Step: Combine all steps into one.

_____

_____

_____

_____

By completing this exercise, you'll learn how to write words unique to your own experience that will capture the attention of your Facebook friends. Tweaking a few words in your approach can make the difference in a friend becoming a customer or distributor for your business.

Completing Your Post

Knowledge Check 5.3
(Circle your answer)

T	F	You want to add a picture of you with a big smile and your products to the post.
T	F	Tag everyone including your sponsor.

Fill In The Blank
Using It To The Utmost

Prior to reading our book, did you tag others or use emotions and actions in your Facebook posts? Why or why not?

_____

_____

_____

Did You Know?
Opt-Out

You can remove yourself if tagged inappropriately at any time.

Insider Tip
Tagging *Works*

Tagging and using the emotion feature might seem like a waste of time.

One of my students had a tough time understanding this idea, as well. However, she did it anyway. As she spoke privately to friends who liked and commented on her post, some of these friends mentioned how the emotion feature stuck out in the newsfeed, causing them to see her post. Other friends spoke about how the person tagged in her post said something in the comments that made them think this might be a great product.

Result? Seven new customers!

Mental Check
Tag Without Fear

Some distributors don't want to tag the more successful distributors because they fear their friends will bypass them and join with the other distributor. If you're working and have a relationship with the successful distributor, you don't have to worry about this. It is in their best interest to help you succeed.

Some distributors choose the most positive smiley faces and emotions because they want to look good. Be yourself. If you're nervous, then choose the nervous feeling under the smiley-face option.

Exercise
Post, Tag & Emote

Let's make sure you understand how to complete your post with a photo, tag and emotions.

Photo: Take three pictures with you and your product. Ask a few friends which picture captures you at your best. Which picture did your friends choose? (write name of picture file below)

_____

Exercise (continued)
Post, Tag & Emote

Photo: Have fun with it. Invite other distributors and have a product photo shoot in your home. Take serious pictures and fun ones. Not only will you have fun bonding with your distributors, but you will also have some amazing photos.

Tag: Make a list of distributors you work with in your upline. It might be the person who introduced you to the business or the person above you who is earning a full-time income as a distributor. Tag these people in your post. You can tag as many people as you want, as long as they are helping you build your business and you have a relationship with them. Whom did you tag?

            1. _____

            2. _____

            3. _____

Emotions: Choose the emotion that best matches how you are feeling at this very moment. Which emotion did you choose? _____

By completing these exercises, you'll be ready to do a "Grand Launch" public post. Make it a goal to do your post in the next 72 hours. Remember, you are just going public. You're not concerned how many respond to this post. We have seen distributors capture more than five new customers with this post while others captured none. It's all in the activity.

Final Thoughts

Instant sales are great for business. A "Grand Launch" public post can make sales happen today.

What are your five biggest takeaways from this chapter?

1. _____

2. _____

3. _____

4. _____

5. _____

NOTES:

Chapter 6

Go Personal On Facebook With Messages

Would you prefer to have a one-on-one or group conversation with a friend about your business?

By being intimate and close with your friend in a one-on-one conversation, you can unravel your friend's pain and show her how your business can give her a better life.

Let's learn how Facebook Messenger grows your business!

Take a few minutes now to reread or skim chapter seven in *Network Marketing For Facebook* before completing this workbook section.

Knowledge Check 6.1		
(Circle your answer)		
T	F	Facebook Messenger allows you to chat with someone in a way similar to email.
T	F	Facebook Messenger conversations disappear automatically after you've had them.
T	F	We recommend you reach out to your existing Facebook friends before contacting new people on Facebook.

Fill In The Blank
Count 'Em Up

How many friends do you currently have on Facebook?

_____

Did You Know?
That's a Lot of People

700 million people use Facebook Messenger each month.

Insider Tip
Don't Prejudge

I hate to admit it, but I used to prejudge my friends early in my network marketing career. I wouldn't talk to a friend if I thought he would not have interest in my company.

One time, I prejudged a doctor friend. I thought he was happy with his career. Eventually, he enrolled as a distributor in my company with someone else. He built a team of tens of thousands of distributors and became a top money earner. I was happy for him, but I missed a huge opportunity because I thought I knew my friend better than he knew himself.

Don't make the same mistake. Contact *all* your Facebook friends.

Mental Check
You Never Know

Do you believe you've already reached out to your Facebook friends? Scroll through your friends list. You might be surprised how many people you haven't contacted.

Fear of rejection is one of the biggest causes of distributor failure. Many distributors with this fear solved the problem by reaching out to successful friends through Facebook Messenger. They found a Facebook connection less risky than a face-to-face meeting, and many of these efforts resulted in new customers and distributors.

Many distributors prejudge, thinking they know which of their friends would be interested in their business. The truth is, a distributor doesn't *really* know.

Does your friend share everything with you?

Your friend might be barely keeping his head above water with bills, yet when you are with him, he is smiling and having the time of his life. Your girlfriend may have a skin condition she doesn't share with others, even her closest friends.

In both examples, friends need a solution to a secret problem. Your product or opportunity might be the answer. What if you don't reach out to them? They may become a customer or distributor with someone else in your company.

Download the Facebook Messenger app onto your smartphone. Communicating with your friends on the go is an easier way to build your business than sitting in front of a computer.

Read the conversations you had with the last 20 people to whom you spoke via Facebook Messenger. Study the entire history of each chat. Overall, are you building relationships or keeping it strictly business? Be honest with yourself.

Collect the name of one new person you meet face to face. Send this person a Facebook Friend Request and a private message via Facebook Messenger. Make it a goal to do this once per week. When it becomes easy, increase your goal to two new people per week. Continue increasing your goal as each week becomes easy. What is the name of your first goal week person? _____

By completing these exercises, you'll learn the importance of sending private messages through Facebook Messenger. People tend to become customers and distributors in a shorter period of time when you talk to them privately.

Before Messaging Your Friends

Knowledge Check 6.2
(Circle your answer)

T	F	If you haven't spoken to someone in the last 90 days, say, "Hey! We haven't spoken in a while. How have you been? By the way, I'm using a weight loss product that helped me lose 15 pounds in a month. Would you like to check it out?"
T	F	If you have spoken to someone recently and have a relationship with her, say, "Hey, Sarah. As you may know, I'm careful with what I put on my skin. I found a wonderful aloe vera-based skincare line. Would you like to try a sample?"

Fill In The Blank
Be Sociable

How many of your existing Facebook friends have you spoken with in the last 90 days using Facebook Messenger? How many *haven't* you spoken with during this same time period?

Spoken To: Not Spoken To:

_____   _____

Did You Know?
First Impressions

At first meet, it takes only seven seconds for one person to judge another person. How you approach a person about business is crucial.

Insider Tip
When to Talk About Your Business

When reestablishing a relationship, your opportunity to talk about your business happens when your friend says, "What have you been up to?" or a similar question about your life.

Ask yourself, "If I send a message to a friend, will she know who I am?" If yes, you might be able to share your business with her right away. If not, reestablish the relationship first.

I used to think I could talk about my business immediately. After all, I was going to change my friends' lives. I experienced a rude awakening when one friend said to me, "Why do I only hear from you when you want me to join your business or try some product?"

Ouch!

It hurt. However, my friend's candor made me realize the importance of relationships.

Mental Check
Warm Up Comes First

Some distributors believe they can immediately talk about their business to a friend they've known for 15 years, even if they haven't spoken to him for a while. Imagine a friend of 15 years reaches out to you on Facebook. You haven't spoken to him in six months, and he immediately launches into selling you on a business opportunity "you just have to participate in!" How would you feel?

Let's make sure you understand what to do before messaging your friends.

You have Facebook friends with whom you have never had a conversation. These are the connections you cannot recall when or how you made Facebook friends.

Find three Facebook friends who fit this description. Send a message to each friend saying, "Hey! I see we haven't spoken on Facebook, yet we are Facebook friends. I wanted to reach out and say hi. I hope we can become friends. How are you?"

Take the extra step and review each friend's Facebook Profile. Add something in your message that is personal to your friend. For example, "I saw a picture on your profile of two beautiful little girls. Are these your daughters? I have two young boys myself."

Which three friends did you choose?

1. _____

2. _____

3. _____

If you haven't spoken to Facebook friends in 90 days, use this opportunity to get to know them better.

Find three Facebook friends who fit this description. Send a message to each friend and say, "Hey! I see we haven't spoken on Facebook in a few months. I wanted to reach out and say hi. I hope we can become better friends. How are you?"

Just like the last exercise, making this message personal goes a long way.

Which three friends did you choose?

1. _____

2. _____

3. _____

If you feel comfortable talking about your business to these individuals on the first message, go for it if it feels right.

Find three real-friend Facebook connections and ask them to check out your business.

Which three friends did you choose?

1. _____

2. _____

3. _____

By completing these exercises, you'll learn how to reach out to Facebook friends based on your relationship with each friend. Contacting a Facebook friend correctly makes a difference if your friend is willing to learn more about your business.

How To Message

Knowledge Check 6.3
(Circle your answer)

T	F	Never use a script *as is*. Always add your personality to it.
T	F	The following is an effective message to send on Facebook Messenger: *Hi! How are you? I hope you are not using harsh chemicals in your home. They cause Cancer! I have something you need to use.* *What's your mailing address so I can shoot you a sample?*
T	F	The following is an effective message to send on Messenger: *Hey! The holidays are coming up and we all put on extra weight. I have a real solution allowing us to eat whatever we want and never gaining a pound. Can I send you a sample?*
T	F	The following is an effective message to send on Messenger: *Do you remember our chat in the past about how you wish your hair had more volume? I found something that might do the trick.* *Would you like a sample?*

Knowledge Check 6.3 (continued)
(Circle your answer)

T	F	The following is an effective message to send on Messenger: *Hi (insert friend's first name)! How are you? You're not going to believe this! My electric bill is now free.*
		Would you like for me to see if I can get you a free electric bill as well?
T	F	The following is an effective message to send on Messenger: *I found the cheapest jewelry and it looks amazing! Do you want to check it out?*
T	F	The following is an effective message to send on Messenger: *Hey! I saw your Facebook post about wanting to save money on your travels. I work with a company that can save you up to 50%.*
		Would you like to check it out?

Fill In The Blank
Follow the Prescription

Write the script we suggested in *Network Marketing for Facebook* , based on your product category.

_____

_____

_____

_____

Edit the script so it fits your personality here:

_____

_____

_____

_____

Did You Know?
Who We Trust

According to Nielson, 84% of consumers say they either completely or somewhat trust recommendations from family and friends about products, making these recommendations the highest ranked for trustworthiness.

The fastest way to acquire a new customer or distributor is to focus on her needs. For example, if your friend wants to lose weight and you have a weight loss product, focus on how the product can help her with weight loss. Talking about how much money she could earn doesn't help with weight loss.

The general rule is to focus on the product first.

If you know someone is hurting financially, don't focus on the product. Customize our script, and focus on the opportunity. For example you can say, "Hi Sarah! How are you? I know you're struggling right now with paying the bills. I found something that could help you earn extra money. I'm doing it myself. Should I send you more information?"

Or after trying a sample, but before your friend is about to pay for the products you can say, "Before you order my products, would you have any interest in getting these same products for free by referring other people to me? Or you might want to earn a part-time or full-time income by sharing these samples with your friends as a distributor? I can show you how to fit this it into your schedule by using Facebook. If not, no biggie. I just wanted to let you know before you paid for the products."

Earlier in my network marketing career, I use to think everyone wanted to become rich. Now, I realize everyone has a unique definition of rich. For some, rich means making millions. For others, rich is earning an extra $1,000 a month to help their child through college.

Many years ago, I had a conversation with a potential distributor. I spoke to him for about an hour about how rich we were going to be from network marketing. After I ran out of things to say, he said, "Jim, I just want to make $5,000 a month so I can quit my job and be a full-time dad. That is rich to me."

Lesson learned.

Mental Check
Tell The Truth

Some distributors have sold in multiple network marketing companies during their career. They tend to get nervous sharing another product and another opportunity with their friends out of fear that their friends may judge them.

As long as you left your last company for ethical reasons, you can be honest with your friends. They'll appreciate your smart business decisions and welcome your new company. In fact, they may value your praise for the new company even more when they hear your wise criticism of the previous company.

As long as you do your due diligence on the product and company, the only reasons you should leave a company are because it went out of business, unethical behaviors from the company itself, or you lost your passion for the product and opportunity.

Exercise
3 Types of Friends

Let's make sure you understand how to message certain types of people.

Recall your last five conversations with your friends about business prior to our training. Answer the questions below.

- Were you friendly, or did it sound like you were trying to sell something?   _____

- Were you talking to your friends the same way you would face to face, with compassion, or were you short with your words and keeping it all about business?   _____

- Did you end each conversation with a question so your friends could tell you yes or no to learning more about your business?   _____

We all have friends who want to earn extra money, who are always looking for opportunities, and who know everyone because these friends are outgoing in the community. Write the names of five friends for each category today. Contact those listed through Facebook Messenger using a version of our making money script you personalized for your personality.

	Earn Money	Looking	Knows Everyone
1.	_____	_____	_____
2.	_____	_____	_____
3.	_____	_____	_____
4.	_____	_____	_____
5.	_____	_____	_____

Now that you made a list of friends who might have an interest in being a distributor, make a list of five new friends who might have an interest in your products today. Contact those listed through Facebook Messenger using a version of our product script you personalized for your personality.

1. _____
2. _____
3. _____
4. _____
5. _____

By completing these exercises, you'll know how to message people based on what these people are looking for in life. Building a successful business is as easy as giving people what they want. You just have to know how to talk to people.

How To Make Hundreds Of Messages More Manageable

Knowledge Check 6.4
(Circle your answer)

T	F	If you are feeling motivated, it's okay to reach out to as many friends as you want in a day.
T	F	Facebook monitors how quickly you contact your friends with similar messages.

Fill In The Blank
Realistic Numbers

Based on your current schedule, how many friends can you reach out to per day through Facebook Messenger? Be realistic. It's not a race. It's more a marathon.

_____

Did You Know?
Pace Yourself

Many people are not consistent because they want success in a few weeks or months. Most successful distributors understand you have to be consistent for years, doing the little things, to see extraordinary success.

Insider Tip
Reaching Out

Before social media became what it is today, distributors didn't have a way to know if their team was working the numbers correctly to be successful as a distributor.

Boy, have times changed.

Today, if I had a team of 10 distributors reaching out to ten friends a day, seven days a week, on Facebook, I know approximately 3,000 people will hear about my business over the next 30 days.

I can show my 10 distributors how to track these numbers so we can make the necessary adjustments and ensure we are enrolling the correct amount of customers and distributors.

So, what are the magic numbers?

At a minimum, distributors should reach out to 10 new friends per day on Facebook. If my distributors had more time, I would advise them to contact 10 new friends every four hours, with no more than 30 per day.

If you do more than I recommend, you might get put into "Facebook Jail" and won't be allowed to reach out to your friends for 30 days.

Facebook wants you to build meaningful relationships, not spam people. Be careful.

Insider Tip (continued)
Reaching Out

Sadly, I have been put in Facebook Jail. These days, I can contact 100 people at a time and not be blocked because I focus on building relationships. Over time, if you become proficient at building relationships, you, too, can increase your numbers. Keep in mind, I have been building relationships the right way on Facebook for years.

Mental Check
Just 10 Minutes A Day

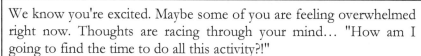

We know you're excited. Maybe some of you are feeling overwhelmed right now. Thoughts are racing through your mind... "How am I going to find the time to do all this activity?!"

Great news! It only takes 10 minutes a day for every 10 friends once you are comfortable with the process. Can you find 10 minutes a day to change your life forever?

We think you can.

Exercise
Two Accountability Partners

Let's make sure you understand how to make hundreds of messages more manageable.

Hold yourself accountable. Fill in the blanks today.

I will reach out to _____ friends per day through Facebook Messenger. I will not miss a day because of my why. My why is

_____ .

Someone else should hold you accountable to your commitment above. Choose this person. Write his or her name. _____

Reach out to 10 Facebook friends. Time yourself. How long did it take? _____

Once you can consistently contact 10 Facebook friends a day with little effort. increase the amount to 20 Facebook friends. How long does it take now? _____

Are you ready to stretch yourself? Once contacting 20 Facebook friends becomes easy, increase the number to 30. Remember, make each message unique and more than four hours apart from each other. How long does it take now? _____

By completing these exercises, you'll effectively reach out to all of your existing Facebook friends in the shortest time period. Once you master your time, duplicate these exercises with your distributors, potentially exposing your business to thousands of new people in the next 30 days.

What Kind of Results Should You Expect?

		Knowledge Check 6.5 (Circle your answer)
T	F	This is not a numbers game. It's about closing people by using sales techniques.
T	F	Finding that one big leader who joins as a distributor in your business is the key to success.
T	F	Some friends may not be interested and don't feel the need to respond to your messages.
T	F	Some friends don't respond to your Facebook message because they may not be interested but didn't want you to feel bad and thought no response was more polite than replying with a "no."

Fill In The Blank
Progress

In the last 30 days, how many people have you spoken to about your business?

_____

Did You Know?
Know Your Numbers

Every successful business in every industry around the world succeeds when that business understands the numbers required to be successful for its industry and company.

Insider Tip
Consistency

Your success isn't determined by who becomes a customer or distributor; rather, success means doing the small, daily stuff over and over again. Persistent daily activity determines your success.

I find that friends don't respond to my Facebook Message when I don't have a real relationship with them, when they miss my message because they are sidetracked with something else, or when they don't check messages often.

One of the small, daily tasks is working the numbers.

If I were a distributor today, my numbers might look like the following.

- I have 2,000 Facebook friends.

- I did not contact 400 of these friends for one reason or another. We all have those types of friends. Maybe they are in the same network marketing company or already a customer or distributor on my team.

- Out of the 1,600 remaining, 900 didn't respond at all. Most likely, I don't really have a relationship with them yet.

- Of the 700 who did respond, 400 wanted a sample. I'm excited!

- Out of the 400 who wanted a sample, 225 reviewed additional information. Everyone wants free samples, so I would make them watch a video or check out a website before sending a sample.

- Out of the 225 who received samples, 34 became customers and 21 distributors. Success!

By keeping track of my numbers, I know my success rate. I know the industry statistic is 1 out of every 20 people to whom you speak about your product will become a distributor. In this example, I spoke to 700. I also know, for my company, 1 out of 5 people who try a sample will become a customer. In this example, that number is 225.

To determine if I am being successful, I start with the number 700. These are the people who interacted with me by saying yes or no to checking out my business. I don't count the other 1,300 because I have not had a conversation with them.

Based on my company and industry statistics, I should have 45 new customers out of 225 people and 35 new distributors out of 700.

However, I have 34 customers and 21 distributors. I know I'm doing something wrong, and now I can improve myself.

Without understanding these numbers, how can you possibly know if you are doing well? This is a hypothetical but accurate example based on industry statistics and what I observe every day on Facebook with my students.

It's easy to be stressed and feel like you're failing when you focus on things over which you have no control. Control your business by talking to new people. You have no control over the decisions of others. Simply move on to the next person.

Exercise
Expectations

Let's make sure you know what kind of results you should expect.

Keep track of your numbers by filling in the blanks below.

- I have _____ Facebook friends.

- I did not contact _____ of these friends for one reason or another. We all have those types of friends. Maybe they are in the same network marketing company or already a customer or distributor on your team.

- Out of the _____ remaining, _____ didn't respond at all. Most likely, I don't yet have a relationship with them.

- Of the _____ who did respond, _____ wanted a sample. I'm excited!

- Out of the _____ who wanted a sample, _____ reviewed additional information. Everyone wants free samples. Make each friend watch a video or check out a website before sending a sample.

- Out of the _____ to whom I sent samples, _____ became customers and _____ distributors. Success!

- By keeping track of numbers, I know if I'm doing well. I know the industry statistic is 1 out of every 20 people will become a distributor. I spoke to _____. I also know, for my company, 1 out of _____ people who try a sample becomes a customer.

- To determine if I'm successful or not, I start with the number _____. These are the people who interacted with me by saying yes or no to checking out my business. I don't count the other _____ because I have not yet had a conversation with these friends.

- Based on my company and industry statistics, I should have _____ new customers out of _____ people and _____ new distributors out of _____.

By completing this exercise, you'll know how your numbers compare to your company and industry statistics. By understanding what you should expect, you will know where you must improve to be a successful distributor.

Final Thoughts

Do you believe you should go personal on Facebook with messages?

It's important to approach your friends the right way the first time by understanding your relationship with your friends, what to say, how frequently you should contact your friends, and what kind of results should you expect.

What are your five biggest takeaways from this chapter?

1. _____

2. _____

3. _____

4. _____

5. _____

NOTES:

Chapter 7

How To Respond When Friends Message Back

H ow do you feel when a friend has an interest in your business? It's probably the same feeling you had when you realized your company could change your life for the better.

You're excited. However, make sure your friend is really interested in your business by giving him additional information.

Let's learn how having a conversation in Facebook Messenger grows your business.

Take a moment now to refresh your knowledge of chapter eight in *Network Marketing For Facebook*. Then complete this workbook section.

Knowledge Check 7.1		
(Circle your answer)		
T	F	Giving additional information is especially important for you if you'll be sending samples.
T	F	By giving people additional information to review before sending out a sample, you still might not improve your sales conversion rate.
T	F	A customer testimonial photo album from your company's Facebook Business Page is solid information you can give your friend to review before sending a sample.
T	F	Your personal profile is a great piece of additional information you can give your friend prior to sending a sample.

Fill In The Blank
Write It Down

What types of additional information do you currently use to qualify someone before sending a sample of your product?

_____

_____

_____

_____

Did You Know?
That's a Lot of Talking

Every hour, nine million messages are sent via Facebook.

Insider Tip
Sending Messages

If your company is set up correctly on Facebook then the Facebook Photo Albums from your company's Facebook Business Page are solid pieces of information to share with your friends during this step.

Sometimes it's okay to send a sample without having your friend review additional information. I recommend you only skip the additional information step if you are face-to-face friends with him, and you believe he will appreciate your products.

In 2014, I worked with a start-up network marketing company. The company hired me to train and coach their distributors. Distributors who sent samples without additional information obtained 1 out of 15 people as customers. Distributors who provided additional information converted 1 out of 5 people into to customers.

Mental Check
Hold Your Horses

As a distributor, you are excited when someone expresses interest in your products. You might want to send samples before your friend really looked into your products, thinking it will be a motivation to become a customer or distributor faster. Sending samples prematurely or sending many samples does *not* guarantee results.

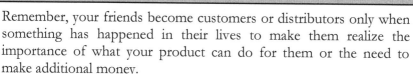

Remember, your friends become customers or distributors only when something has happened in their lives to make them realize the importance of what your product can do for them or the need to make additional money.

Stick to our recommended process, and you'll see your business flourish.

Exercise
3 Steps to a Successful Response

Let's make sure you know how to respond when friends message back.

Writing a successful response takes three easy steps.

Step 1: Thank your friend for responding to your message. Write how you would thank your friend below.

_____

_____

_____

Step 2: Give some information. The best types of information are company marketing videos, customer testimonials, and product details. Write how you would present the information to your friend below.

_____

_____

_____

Step 3: Let your friend know the next step she should take. Insert your next step here:

_____

_____

_____

Final Step: Combine all steps into one.

_____

_____

_____

_____

_____

_____

Contact distributors with whom you are working and ask, "What are the best types of information I can share with my friends to get them excited about being a customer or distributor?" What did these distributors say?

_____

_____

By completing these exercises, you'll know how to respond to your friends in a professional way that helps them make an educated decision on being a customer or distributor. As we said many times throughout our training, saying the right things at the right time can make all the difference.

Follow Up

T	F	It's okay to send a sample, even if they don't respond to your messages. They'll love your product and become a customer if they just try it.
T	F	If a friend isn't responding to your messages, it's okay to follow up with them as many times as you like in a week.
T	F	If a friend doesn't respond to your message quickly, it doesn't mean he isn't interested. People get busy, and some don't look at their Facebook daily.

Fill In The Blank
Follow-Up Plan

If your friend isn't responding, how many times do you currently follow up with her and for how long? For example you might say, "I follow up with her every 2 days for a month."

Did You Know?
A Good Business Habit

Most people don't follow up in any type of business, not just in the network marketing profession. The most successful people in every industry are professionals who follow up.

Insider Tip
I Said No at First

My 20-year career in the network marketing profession and social media almost didn't happen.

I was contacted by a friend to become a distributor for a network marketing company in February of 2011. I kindly declined, saying, "I'm busy with college and my job. Stay in touch, though."

My friend followed up about a month later. I still had the same reason; however, he gave me some additional information and asked when he could call me back. For whatever reason, I told him one month.

One month later, he contacted me as he said he would. Two interesting things happened this time that inspired me to sign up as a distributor for his company.

First, my college semester was ending, so I had extra time. Second, he said I could work hands-on with Mark Yarnell. Mark is one of the most successful network marketing distributors in the history of our profession. I chatted with Mark. Within a few days, I enrolled as a distributor. This company catapulted me from amateur to professional in network marketing.

What if my friend had decided not to follow up two separate times over a period of 60 days? I might not be here teaching you how to be successful with Facebook.

You may not follow up because it feels pushy, because you forget, or because you prejudged people the first time you spoke with them about the business. Consider the following counterpoints to your reasoning.

Feels pushy:	If you are a professional, you are highly unlikely to come across as pushy. By following our suggestions, you won't follow up too frequently or turn them off by the tone of your message.
You forget:	You are busy. You have a full-time job, family, and hobbies. Using your phone calendar to schedule follow-ups is powerful because you will be notified of the follow up without needing to remember. As you send messages through Facebook Messenger you can keep your message unread until you have followed up with your friend three times.
Prejudge the people:	Just because someone isn't responding or says no right now doesn't mean this person will say no forever. Look at the Insider Tip above as a great example.

Exercise
3 Steps to Successful Follow Up

Let's make sure you understand how to follow up.

Writing a successful follow up takes three easy steps.

Step 1: Tell your friend why you are sending a message. For example, "Hey! You mentioned you wanted to try my products." Write a similar response below, in your own words, so your friend knows it's you talking, not a script you copied and pasted.

_____

_____

_____

Step 2: Ask a question. For example, "Did you have a chance to check out … ?" Write a similar response below in your own words, adding the information you asked your friend to review.

_____

_____

_____

Step 3: Tell your friend what happens next. For example, "Let me know, and I will drop a sample in the mail. I can't wait to hear from you. Thanks!" Write a similar response below in your own words.

_____

_____

_____

Final Step: Combine all steps into one.

_____

_____

_____

_____

_____

By completing this exercise, you'll have a better response when following up with your friends. Following up is a crucial step to becoming a successful distributor.

Your Friend Said, "No" To A Sample

Knowledge Check 7.3
(Circle your answer)

T	F	If handled properly, most will say yes within six months.
T	F	Place any friends who respond no in a friends list called Prospects.
T	F	If a friend says no, stop spending your time with him and focus on others who might say yes.
T	F	Friends go into a Prospect list as long as your friends respond back to your message with a yes or no.

Fill In The Blank
You Know People

How many friends are currently in your Prospect list?

_____

Did You Know?
Why "No" Is Good

Successful distributors in the network marketing profession believe that someone's no gets them closer to a yes. Rather than feeling defeated or rejected, consider your proximity to a yes down the road.

Insider Tip
The Power of Lists

Before Mark Yarnell taught me how to understand the numbers, it was easy to feel bummed when friends said no to me. I took it personally. Don't focus on the no responses. Focus on the activity of asking others if they want a sample. You can't control people's responses. You can control how many people with whom you speak.

I have had over 11,000 people say no to me throughout my career. I still enrolled 600 distributors, and lived the life I always dreamed of since being a kid.

Lists are a great way to organize your friends and interests, to sort your News Feed, and reach (or exclude) specific people when sharing things on Facebook. Your lists are unique to you. With lists, you can see what's going on with all of your favorite sports teams or announce a garage sale to friends in your current city.

You can create as many friends lists as you want.

For example, you might make a list called 'name of your network marketing company'. This is different from your Team list, which contains people you signed up below you. This alternate list contains anyone else you meet in your company, if you build a relationship with them.

You may also choose to create lists based on where you meet your friends. For example, you may have lists called Chicago and Austin.

Be creative. This is your way of staying organized on Facebook.

Mental Check
"No" Is Actually, Surprisingly, *Normal*

Everyone receives no's throughout life. Here are three examples.

You might have a child. Has your child ever said no to you? Probably a 100 times a day. Did that make you want to stop being a parent?

Maybe you are married or in a happy relationship. Didn't you hear the word no a few times before you met that special someone?

Think about friends. Have you ever invited a friend to lunch and she said no?" Did you stop being a friend with her?

In these three examples, you moved forward because you didn't take the rejection personally. The same mentality will benefit you in business. Just realize what you have to offer isn't for everyone.

Exercise
3 Steps to Successfully Responding to "No"

Let's make sure you understand what to do when a friend says no to a sample.

Writing a successful response takes three easy steps.

Step 1: Show your friend the relationship is more important than trying a sample. For example, "Okay, no problem!" In your own words, how would you say it?

_____

_____

_____

Step 2: Show appreciation. For example, "Thanks for getting back to me." In your own words, how would you say it?

_____

_____

_____

Step 3: Focus on the relationship. For example, "How have you been?" In your own words, how would you say it?

_____

_____

_____

Final Step: Combine all steps into one.

_____

_____

_____

_____

Sometimes it feels right to dig a little deeper when a friend says no to a sample. For example, if you are selling skincare products, you can say, "Okay, no problem! Thanks for getting back to me. How have you been? Also, may I ask what skincare you are using now and what you love about it? This will help me when talking to other people." Write a response that digs deeper, based on your product.

_____

_____

_____

_____

By completing these exercises, you'll know how to respond to those who say no to trying a sample in a way that will keep your friend as a potential customer in the future. You'll also learn how to dig a little deeper if it makes sense. Handling rejection in a professional way turns that same rejection into a yes with proper follow up.

Your Friend Said, "Yes" To A Sample

T	F	If handled properly, most people who say yes will become a customer after they receive the sample.
T	F	After he says yes, put your friend in a friends list called Sample.
T	F	Friends go into a Sample list as long as your friends say yes to trying a sample the first time you speak with them..

Fill In The Blank
Write It Down

How many friends are currently in your Sample list?

_____

Did You Know?
Look At All These Happy Customers

A great piece of information to include during the sample phase is a customer testimonial Facebook photo album from your company's Facebook Business Page.

Insider Tip
Just Try It

I love hearing the word yes! Remember, your friend only agreed to try a sample. Your friend still has to try it and see if your product is a fit for their life.

When crafting your message to send to a friend after she has tried a sample, always include your company's monthly product promotion or something that makes your potential customer feel she is getting deals and savings whenever possible.

Mental Check
Don't Count Your Chickens

It's best not to get overly excited when a friend requests a sample. Some will not move forward as a customer or distributor after trying the sample.

If your company has a one out of five sample-to-customer conversion, it means four people who tried a sample did not move forward.

These people may have not liked the price, the ingredients, or the way the product made them feel.

Keep your emotions neutral, and treat this like a business.

Let's make sure you understand what to do when a friend says yes to a sample.

Writing a successful response takes just two steps.

Step 1: Tell your friend the sample was sent. For example, "Hey! I just sent out your sample." In your own words, how would you say it?

_____

_____

_____

Step 2: Give your friend an assignment with the sample. For example, "Let me know what you think after you try it." In your own words, how would you say it?

_____

_____

_____

Final Step: Combine both steps into one.

_____

_____

_____

_____

Now it's time to ask for the sale. Remember, not all samples turn into customers. Writing a successful response takes three easy steps.
Step 1: Ask a question. For example, "Hey! How are you enjoying the sample? Let me know if you have any questions." How would you say it?

_____

_____

_____

Step 2: Give your friend a reason to become a customer today. For example, "I wanted to let you know about this month's product promotion. It is ...." How would you say it?

_____

_____

_____

Step 3: Show your friend how to become a customer. For example, "The website to order is .... Just click on ... to take advantage of the promotion. Look forward to hearing from you." How would you say it?

_____

_____

_____

Final Step: Combine all steps into one.

_____

_____

_____

_____

Sometimes it feels right to dig a little deeper when a friend says yes to a sample, but doesn't become a customer or distributor. For example, if you are selling a weight loss product, you can say, "Thanks for trying the sample. I really appreciate it. May I ask why you decided not to become a customer after you tried the sample? What did you like and dislike about the product? People are losing weight, including myself, so I just want to make sure I address your concerns. Your answers will help me as I talk to other people." Write a response that digs deeper based on your product.

_____

_____

_____

_____

_____

By completing these exercises, you'll know how to respond to those who said yes to trying a sample, how to motivate these people to become a customer, and how to dig deeper when it makes sense. Many times a distributor turns off their friends because the distributor is aggressive. There is a difference between being aggressive and thorough.

Your Friend Hasn't Responded To The Sample Offer

		Knowledge Check 7.5 (Circle your answer)
T	F	Until he or she becomes a customer or say no, send a friendly message three times a week.
T	F	Here is an example of an effective follow up message: *Hey! I sent you a message last week. How are you enjoying the samples?*
T	F	Here is an example of an effective follow up message: *Hey! Did you have a chance to place your order? I want to make sure you don't miss out on this once-in-a-lifetime product and opportunity.*
T	F	Here is an example of an effective follow up message: *Hey! I'm surprised you haven't responded to my messages. Can you at least have the courtesy to get back with me? I would appreciate hearing from you.*

Fill In The Blank
Put Yourself In Their Shoes

From your own experiences, why do you think some of your friends didn't respond to you after you sent a sample?

_____

_____

_____

Did You Know?
It's Not Up To You

People move forward as a customer or distributor when they choose, not when you choose.

A friend asked if I would like to sample her product. Even though I'm no longer a distributor, I love to support our profession by being a customer of products that make my life better.

I said yes.

She reached out to me three times before I was able to let her know if I would be a customer. Was I ignoring her? No. I was traveling the country, doing Facebook events, so I was busy. Eventually, I responded. Now she has a new customer.

We never know why people are not responding to our messages. All we can do is be professional and stay in touch.

Also, there are a number of ways you can mistakenly turn people off when following up with them. People can easily misunderstand you online. That's why it's so important to be genuine and positive.

I suggest using a normal, non-salesy, non-marketing, conversational language, or people will feel you don't really care about them as a person.

Always watch how you phrase things when you feel frustrated. If you become negatively emotional in any way—for example, if you feel frustrated about a lack of progress in network marketing—it's a good time to step away from the computer and smartphone for a while. Come back later and rethink your communications.

Remember, if your friend becomes a customer, move her from the Sample list to the Customer list. Your friend should never be in more than one list at a time.

Mental Check
Don't Assume

You may feel one of the following if a friend doesn't respond back to you after trying a sample.

She doesn't like the product: You don't know if she had the opportunity to try the product yet. It's best not to assume what she did or didn't do unless she told you directly.

No one will like the product: You shouldn't believe everyone wouldn't like your product based on one person. There are plenty of others in your area who will like your product as much as you do.

Mental Check (continued)
Don't Assume

Maybe this isn't a good company to become a distributor. If you believe in the product and others believe in the product and are making an income sharing it with others, keep searching. There isn't one company in the world where everyone uses their product.

Exercise
How to Get a Response to Your Sample

Let's make sure you understand what to do if your friend hasn't responded to the sample offer.

Writing a successful response takes just two steps.

Step 1: Opening statement. For example, "Hey! I sent you a message last week." or "Hey! Thanks for trying the samples." In your own words, how would you say it?

_____

_____

_____

Step 2: Ask a question. For example, "How are you enjoying the samples?" or "Did you have a chance to place your order?" In your own words, how would you say it?

_____

_____

_____

Final Step: Combine both steps into one.

_____

_____

_____

_____

_____

By completing this exercise, you'll know how to respond to those who have not yet replied to your sample offer. People get busy. Stay in touch in a friendly manner, and watch your friends become customers and distributors.

Knowledge Check 7.6
(Circle your answer)

T	F	The following is a life experience that could change your friend's mind about being a customer for your product: Mary says no to trying a sample from you. Two weeks later, her youngest daughter becomes sick after swallowing liquid found in a bottle under the kitchen sink. Her daughter recovers. However, Mary realizes she needs natural alternatives to her chemical-based home products.
T	F	The following is a life experience that could change your friend's mind about being a customer for your product: Gene says no to trying a sample from you. A few months later, he has a heart attack. The doctor informs him because the heart attack was the result his eating habits. He notices you lost 20 pounds since the last time you spoke because you used your product every day.
T	F	The following is a life experience that could change your friend's mind about being a customer for your product: Donna says no to saving money on her electricity bill. Every week you send her a message on Facebook Messenger, sharing with her how she is missing out on the savings. You send her copies of your bill and customer testimonials.
T	F	The following is a life experience that could change your friend's mind about being a customer for your product: Katie says no to checking out all the great travel deals from your company. Every month you send her a Facebook message with a new travel deal, showing her how she is missing out on all the best travel around the world.

Fill In The Blank
Minds Change

From your own experiences, write about a time someone said no and later said yes to looking at your business. What happened in your friend's life that changed her mind?

_____

_____

Did You Know?
I'm Having a Moment

The definition of a "defining moment" in your life is an event that changed the way you think about things.

Insider Tip
It's Only a Matter of Time

As you've learned, a friend will become a customer or distributor when she is ready.

As long as I stay in touch with my friend, it's only a matter of time before she will want to earn some extra money or use my product.

Think about your history. Were you always open to being a distributor in network marketing? In 2001, it took my friend several months of staying in touch with me before I was ready to become a distributor in his company. I'm glad he never gave up on me. That company made me a network marketing professional and set me up for where I am today.

Mental Check
It's Their Timing, Not Yours

Everyone moves forward at his own pace based on life's circumstances. Here are three examples based on examples we used earlier in this chapter.

You might have a child. You can't force your child to eat until she is hungry. However, when your child is ready, she will quickly eat what you have to offer her.

Maybe you are married or in a happy relationship. Perhaps your partner was in an existing relationship when you met. However, you decided to stay in touch until she was available.

Think about friends. Your friend hasn't returned your phone call in two weeks. When you do hear from her, she informs you of her busy days with work and college. However, now that her schedule is clear you will hear from her often.

In these three examples, each person could only move forward when the timing was right in his or her life.

Do this activity while waiting for the no's to be ready.

It's easy to lose touch with those who are not interested in sampling, being a customer, or enrolling as a distributor. Staying in touch with your friends until each one is ready to move forward is done easily if your friends are sorted properly in a Facebook list. Fill in the blanks below.

- How many of your friends are in a Prospect Friend List? _____

- How many of your friends are in a Sample Friend List? _____

- How many of your friends are in a Customer Friend List? _____

- How many of your friends are in a Team Friend List? _____

If you created custom Facebook Friend Lists, please fill in the blanks below.

- How many of your friends are in a _____ Friend List? _____

- How many of your friends are in a _____ Friend List? _____

- How many of your friends are in a _____ Friend List? _____

By completing this exercise, you'll easily manage your Facebook friends and not lose one during the critical time between first hearing about your business and taking action.

Final Thoughts

Do you believe in responding when friends message back?

Knowing how to respond in every situation and regardless of what they say, will determine whether your friends do business with you or someone else.

Being a laid-back and low-pressure professional with your friends gives them a positive experience with you and your business. Then it becomes a matter of time before someone becomes a customer or distributor.

What are your five biggest takeaways from this chapter?

1. _____

2. _____

3. _____

4. _____

5. _____

NOTES:

Chapter 8

How To Turn Customers Into Distributors

S houldn't there be an easy way to transition customers to distributors? After all, if a customer loves your products, it's only natural he will share the products with their friends and family.

Let's reward your customers, financially, when they share your products by helping them become a distributor.

Let's learn how Facebook Group and Messenger work together to grow your business.

Take a few minutes now to reread or skim chapter nine in *Network Marketing For Facebook* before completing this workbook section.

		Knowledge Check 8.1 (Circle your answer)
T	F	All of your customers should be pushed into becoming a distributor because they already believe in your products.
T	F	If your friend becomes a distributor, move her from the Customers to Team friends list in your Facebook account.

Fill In The Blank Sneak Peek
If someone is interested in becoming a distributor, we suggest you add her to your company or leader's Facebook Group. Please reread chapter four in *Network Marketing for Facebook* to understand how to introduce her into the group. How many people in the last 30 days have you added to your Facebook Group? _____

Insider Tip
Success Requires Belief

Becoming a distributor in the network marketing profession is one of the best things people can do to better their lives.

With this being said, someone doesn't need to become a distributor in order for you to be successful.

Many people will refer their friends to you if they can get the product for free. This generates a list of potential customers and distributors. Talking to a strong referral is better than talking to a stranger. Every company is different, but many times this is accomplished via a Facebook or Home Party or Refer a Friend Program.

I don't recommend pressuring a friend into becoming a distributor. This is one of the biggest pitfalls of our profession.

If you want to get rich in network marketing, it requires the same type of work ethic and commitment required in any entrepreneurial activity. Friends who ignore this message will quit network marketing within 90 days. An unsuccessful friend will tell her friends that network marketing doesn't work.

Wouldn't you rather your friend remain a satisfied customer and continue to tell her friends how she loves your product?

My most passionate and committed distributors believed in the product and understood what was required to be a successful distributor before joining my company.

Quality wins over quantity when it comes to enrolling distributors.

Mental Check
Most People Need The Money

Most bankruptcies in the United States would never happen if the family earned just a few extra hundred dollars a month. In fact, 62% of Americans have no emergency savings. Combine this statement with the fact your friend is a satisfied customer, and she'll be more likely to become a distributor.

Exercise
3 Steps to Getting a Distributor

Let's make sure you understand how to turn customers into distributors.

Writing a successful message takes just three steps.

Step 1: Open statement or question. For example, "Hey! How are you enjoying the products?" In your own words, how would you say it?

_____

_____

_____

Step 2: Ask question. For example, "Would you have an interest sharing these products on Facebook for some extra money? It, literally, takes 20 minutes a day." In your own words, how would you say it?

_____

_____

_____

Step 3: Give information. For example, "We have a Facebook Group where you can learn more and meet people who are earning a part-time and full-time income. Here is the link: (enter link). What do you think?

Final Step: Combine three steps into one.

_____

_____

_____

_____

_____

_____

Some customers won't have an interest in being a distributor because those customers lack confidence. Show these customers how much fun and support is involved. If your company does home or Facebook parties, suggest your customers host a party. If not, reach out to a few of your customer's Facebook friends and ask these friends to try a sample. Show your customers how much you are willing to support.

By completing these exercises, you'll know how to inspire customers. Just asking a question and taking a little initiative are sometimes all it takes.

Final Thoughts

Do you believe customers can become distributors?

It can be awkward asking your customers if they would like to make extra money as a distributor, or at the least, refer you to some of their friends, but Facebook Groups and Messenger quickly help people make a decision on this topic.

Personal product testimonials make for a strong story to share with others who know, like, and trust you. These stories hit home because of the relationship between you and your friends. Many of these friends eventually become customers or distributors.

Doesn't it make sense to ask your customers if they have an interest in sharing a product they love with their friends?

What are your five biggest takeaways from this chapter?

1. _____

2. _____

3. _____

4. _____

5. _____

NOTES:

Chapter 9

Why It's Critical To Stay In Touch With Friends

What if we told you there was an easy way to stay in touch with every person you met for the rest of your life?

Besides having many friends, you'd have a huge list of people always wanting to try your product or earn extra money by becoming a distributor in your company.

Let's learn how Newsfeed on Facebook grows your business.

Take a few moments now to re-acquaint yourself with chapter 10 in *Network Marketing For Facebook*. Then complete the exercises in this workbook section.

		Knowledge Check 9.1 *(Circle your answer)*
T	F	A primary way of staying in touch is playing games with your friends on Facebook.
T	F	It's best to post quality content over quantity.
T	F	A smart way to stay in touch with your friends on Facebook is by interacting with your friends' posts.

Fill In The Blank
I Just Call... to Say...

List your favorite ways to stay in touch with friends on Facebook.

_____

_____

_____

Did You Know?
Facebook Connects Us

67% of people use Facebook to stay in touch with current friends.

In 2009, I was a distributor for a network marketing company, growing a team of 350 distributors and doing $110,000 in sales within four months.

People wondered how I was able to achieve such a feat so quickly.

Using social media, I've been staying in touch with people since 1995. One of these people was Ricky. I contacted him through social media to ask if he would have an interest in checking out what I was doing.

A few weeks later, Ricky enrolled as a distributor. He also enrolled a friend from Miami. Ricky's friend was responsible for building a team of 250 distributors (70% of my team). Staying in touch always pays off, as long as you are focused on building relationships and not looking at people as a way to make money.

Most distributors only focus on who wants to be a customer or distributor right now. If this had been my mindset, I never would've stayed in touch with Ricky. This is one of the reasons some distributors never achieve their financial goals in our profession. Most friends won't become a customer or distributor the first time you speak with them.

Fortune is in the follow up. If you don't stay in touch until your friend has a life experience that leads him to your product, he will order your products or become a distributor with someone else—someone who did follow up.

Imagine that one of your friends says no to joining your business as a distributor. Six months later, your friend realizes he needs to make extra money. You decided not to stay in touch with him after his initial no.

Another friend of his happens to be in your company, and this friend did stay in touch with him on Facebook. He joins your company, but with the other friend. A few years later, you see your friend who said no to you walk across the stage at a national convention, being promoted to the highest position in the company. How would that make you feel?

Insider Tip (continued)
Stay in Touch

If a friend doesn't become a customer or distributor right away but he likes everything about your company, it could mean one of two things.

1. First, you don't have the relationship you thought you did with him. Does your friend really know, like, and trust you? Are you really friends?

2. Possibly, your friend hasn't yet had the right life experience. An action-provoking life experience is when someone has an event in his life that makes him realize he needs your product or opportunity.

Mental Check
Trust Takes Time

Some of your Facebook friends may need you to build a relationship with them for the next 12 months before they'll want to consider your product or opportunity. We all have a few Facebook friends that we don't know well, yet somehow they are in our list. Trust happens over time.

For those we do know well, maybe those friends don't yet see the value in your product or opportunity. One day those friends might change their minds. Be there, ready to help.

The most successful distributors in the network marketing profession believe that staying in touch while building strong relationships is one of the pieces to success.

Exercise
How Active Are You?

Let's make sure you understand why it's critical to stay in touch with friends.

Return to your Facebook history to get a true numbers picture of how long it has been since you contacted some people when posting quality content or interacting with your friends' posts. In the last 30 days, count the total number of interactions found in your Facebook history. What is the number?

_____

By completing this exercise, you'll learn if you have been staying in touch with friends on Facebook. Staying in touch allows you to build meaningful relationships until your friends are ready to move forward as a customer or distributor.

Balancing Personal and Business

		Knowledge Check 9.2 (Circle your answer)
T	F	The best way to do a Facebook post is to use the same language you would use with someone over the phone or face to face.
T	F	A Facebook post with a picture or video will get less interaction because your friends won't read the text that goes along with it.
T	F	If you posted once a day on Facebook, seven days a week, a productive week would contain five posts about your business and two personal.
T	F	An example of a personal post might be: A sweet memory this morning at 7 a.m. was staring into my son's eyes as he desperately tried to talk in complete sentences to me ... I only heard—Ba Ball BBB G ... (picture of my son)
T	F	An example of a personal post might be: Am I the only one who loves taking pictures of restaurant bathrooms? Maybe I just admire the creativity. (picture of a bathroom)
T	F	An example of a personal post might be: Life is hard sometimes ... Just Thai. Anyone else like this food? (picture of Thai food).

Fill In The Blank Are You Sharing?
Write your most important personal and business events over the last 12 months. Circle the ones you shared with your friends on Facebook. _____ _____ _____ _____ _____ _____ _____ _____ _____ _____ _____ _____

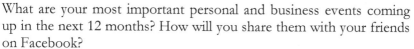

What are your most important personal and business events coming up in the next 12 months? How will you share them with your friends on Facebook?

_____ _____ _____ _____ _____ _____

_____ _____ _____ _____ _____ _____

Did You Know?
Balance

Your success in the network marketing profession is no different than everyday life. Not having balance will eventually hurt you.

Insider Tip
Building Relationships

Do the most successful distributors in your company place a high importance on building relationships with people? I believe the answer is yes.

However, what is a relationship? In my opinion, a relationship is when two people genuinely like each other because they have similar interests, hobbies, or some sort of connection.

The only way to create this connection is by letting others into your life so these people can get to know you.

If I do a Facebook post showing pictures of where I eat, a favorite quote, my family, or something important to me, won't that allow you to learn more about me? And won't that give you an opportunity to find a connection? If you find a connection, doesn't that mean we might become friends?

When I meet someone face to face or phone or video chat for the first time after being friends with him on Facebook for a while, he may say things like: your son is growing up so fast from the pictures I see on Facebook; I love watching your life unfold on Facebook; and I've been watching you talk about your business.

At that point, I know this person knows, likes, and trusts me, as well as respects me as an entrepreneur.

Do you think we will do business together?

Mental Check
You Control Your Privacy

If you take advantage of privacy settings on your posts, only your Facebook friends will see your personal life. If you're still nervous, ask yourself if you would be friends with these people outside of Facebook.

Exercise
Balance

Let's make sure you understand how to balance personal and business.

It's time to brainstorm how you can balance your week between personal and business posts. Today, jot notes about what you might want to post each day.

Monday: _____

_____

Tuesday: _____

_____

Wednesday: _____

_____

Thursday: _____

_____

Friday: _____

_____

Saturday: _____

_____

Sunday: _____

_____

By completing this exercise, you'll learn that balancing your posts between personal and business is not difficult. Once you start to balance, you will notice more interaction from your friends on your posts. Higher interaction leads to more customers and distributors.

The 80/20 Rule And How It Applies Based On How Much You Post A Day

Knowledge Check 9.3 (Circle your answer)		
T	F	If you post three times a day, that's 21 posts a week. Sixteen should be business and five personal.
T	F	If you post twice per day, that's 10 posts a week. Eight would be personal and two business.

Fill In The Blank
Be Realistic

Based on your schedule, how many times can you post on Facebook per day?

_____

Did You Know?
Save Time & Have More Impact

Economist Vilfredo Pareto came up with the 80/20 principle that assumes most of the results in any situation are determined by the smallest number of causes. Usually, 20% of the things you do produce 80% of the results.

Insider Tip
Following the 80/20 Rule

I didn't always believe in the 80/20 rule.

As you know, I became a distributor for the first time in the 90's. I couldn't have a conversation with a friend without mentioning my business. I was overly excited and believed every friend I had would want to be a customer or distributor.

Even if a friend said no, I thought he still meant yes. I just had to bring it up every time we hung out. Over time, most of my friends decided not to hang out with me anymore. You might be chuckling right now because this happened to you, as well. It happens to the best of us. However, if we are to be professionals, we must act accordingly.

Insider Tip (continued)
Following the 80/20 Rule

One day a close friend of mine needed to make some extra money. As usual, I got very excited and shared my business with him. He politely said no. When I asked my friend why, he said, "I don't want to scare away my friends by doing the business like you." No matter what I said to him after those words, I couldn't change his mind. It's not what we say but what we do that matters.

I learned the hard way about the 80/20 rule. I encourage you to learn from my experience.

Mental Check
Don't Be a One-Trick Pony

Some people get annoyed when their friends post too many pictures of their children. Why? It's one-dimensional. All people know are your children. Strive to be multi-dimensional. Share with friends all aspects of your life so they can get to know you. The same holds true for business.

Exercise
Pareto Calculator

Let's make sure you understand the 80/20 rule and how it applies based on how much you post a day.

Review your Facebook posts for the last 30 days. Count how many posts are personal and how many are business.

Personal: _____   Business: _____

Determine if you're already doing the 80/20 rule. Add the personal and business posts from above. What is your total? Next, take the total and multiply it by 80%. The answer represents how many personal posts you should've done over the last 30 days. What is your answer? For those who love math, here is the formula: P + B x .80 = A

Answer: _____

By completing this exercise, you'll know how to stay within the 80/20 rule by doing an easy calculation each week. As much as you believe in your business, your friends do not want to hear about your business more than 20% of the time. However, your friends do want to hear about what's going on in your life on a personal level 80% of the time.

		Knowledge Check 9.4 (Circle your answer)
T	F	A quick way to find quality business posts is share them from your company's personal profile.
T	F	The following is a successful example of what you can add to a shared company Facebook post. I just love when my little girls spill their juice on the carpet. I been using this product for the last few months, and it works like a charm. If you would like more information, please let me know. *(company post will appear here)*
T	F	The following is a successful example of what you can add to a shared company Facebook post. I know there are many ways to lose weight. This product is working for me. I'm down 10 lbs. and this girl is down 40 lbs. Please let me know if you want more information. *(company post will appear here)*
T	F	The following is a successful example of what you can add to a shared company Facebook post. This Bamboo product rocks! My skin condition is cured. I can get you free product if you refer a few friends to me. Please message me now!!! *(company post will appear here)*
T	F	The following is a successful example of what you can add to a shared company Facebook post. I am excited to be attending my company's convention next month. I'm earning $3,000 a month and I can show you how! It's easy! Check out the post below on the convention details! *(company post will appear here)*
T	F	The following is a successful example of what you can add to a shared company Facebook post. I purchased this piece a week ago for my daughter's wedding. I love it! *(company post will appear here)*

Knowledge Check 9.4 (continued)
(Circle your answer)

| T | F | The following is a successful example of what you can add to a shared company Facebook post.

I haven't stayed at this hotel yet; however, I might with this deal. Anyone else love to travel?
(*company post will appear here*) |

Fill In The Blank
Balance

In the last 30 days, how many company Facebook posts did you share with your friends? How many of them did you make personal?

Total Posts Shared   Posts Made Personal

_____   _____

Did You Know?
Knowledge Check

Every successful network marketing company has quality posts on their Facebook Business Page so distributors can share the posts with friends.

Insider Tip
Quality Business Posts

There are three ways to do quality business posts. Let's figure out which one is best for you.

1. Sharing your company's Facebook posts is the best way to get started. It's as simple as clicking share, typing in a personal message, and clicking share one more time.

2. Some of you are a bit savvier with computers and mobile devices, so you might decide to screenshot or download the image from your company's Facebook post and upload it as your own Facebook post. Always give credit in your post. You will notice more likes and comments by your friends with this type of post over sharing a post.

3. The most effective type of post is writing your own and including personal pictures or videos. These organic posts draw the most likes and comments from friends. Why? People do business with you, so they want to see your success.

A true professional will use all three strategies based on what is needed at the time.

Some distributors are in a hurry, so they'll share a post from the company Facebook Business Page without writing something personal. These types of posts don't see many likes or comments because it looks like an ad to your friend rather than a genuine way of sharing a business you care about with your friends. This will not grow your business.

Always share a company Facebook post with a personal message from you.

Exercise
How To Do It

Let's make sure you know how to share and add to company posts.

Select a Facebook post from your company's Facebook Business Page. Practice writing a personal and heartfelt message below to go along with it. Next, share this Facebook post with the message in your Newsfeed.

_____

_____

_____

_____

_____

By completing this exercise, you'll learn how to make your company Facebook posts personal so your friends don't feel like you are advertising. You might be wondering why we asked you to write the message above instead of typing it directly into Facebook. Handwriting accesses a different part of our brain than typing. You might get different results. Experiment in these pages before moving to the computer.

How Often Should You Post

Knowledge Check 9.5		
(Circle your answer)		
T	F	Post daily.
T	F	The best time to post is in the mornings.
T	F	Always post two hours apart.
T	F	If you want to post three times a day, try one post in the morning, afternoon and evening.

Fill In The Blank
Write It Down

How often do you currently post a week?

_____

Did You Know?
Quality Beats Quantity

It's not about how often you should post, rather the quality of each post you share with friends.

Insider Tip
Oversharing

Why do you have this insatiable appetite to post many times throughout the day about your business? At one time, I was so excited about my business, I wanted everyone to hear about it. I thought if I kept changing up a few words or shared different types of information, I might change my friends' minds.

But what if your friends haven't yet tried your products or attended a company event. Most people have been raised to believe the old adage *If it's too good to be true then it probably is.* Your friends will tune out your excitement and believe it to be hype. Remember, a friend is only interested when he has a life experience.

One of my students posted more than five times a day on Facebook about his business and hardly received a like or comment on his posts. Without likes and comments, he never had the opportunity to follow up with people about his business.

Within 45 days of making adjustments based on my feedback, he started to receive likes and comments. This simple change in his business has allowed him to average $200 a month in retail sales.

Mental Check
One Good Post Per Day

In most cases, posting once a day can make you as successful as those who post many times a day. Not only are singular, daily posts usually higher in quality, but a distributor can stay consistent every day for a long period of time with one post. Sometimes a distributor will post many times in a day then go a day with no posts or several days with poor posts.

Quality over quantity wins every time.

Exercise
Posting For A Week

Let's make sure you understand how often to post.

For the next seven days, post once every morning between 8am – 9am in your time zone. Total the number of likes and comments you received on the seven posts: _____

Once you finished with seven days of morning posts, try posting once in the afternoon between 2pm – 4pm in your time zone for seven days. Total the number of likes and comments you received on these seven posts: _____

When your seven days of afternoon posts are completed, post once in the evening between 6pm and 8pm in   for seven days. Total the number of likes and comments you received on these seven posts:

_____

Circle the time period you received the most likes and comments. Most distributors experience higher numbers in the evening. However, quite a few distributors experience higher numbers in alternate time zones.

Morning   Afternoon   Evening

Once you have completed the exercise above, do the following in the time block that gave you the most likes and comments. Do two posts a day for seven days. Most importantly, make sure you post two hours apart. For example, post once at 6pm and again at 8pm.

Did you average more likes and comments per post when you posted once a day or twice a day? _____

By completing these exercises, you'll know what time of day to post if you are going to post once a day. If you are going to post more than once a day, you will know which time is second and third to optimize interaction. You'll also learn why it's important to post more than four hours apart. Knowing how often to post will allow you to post quality over quantity so more posts touch the hearts of your friends. This brings deeper friendships and lasting customers and distributors.

Replying To Posts And Comments

		Knowledge Check 9.6 (Circle your answer)
T	F	When someone comments on your personal post, you don't have to like or comment back.
T	F	When someone comments on your business post, like or comment back within thirty minutes.
T	F	The more you interact with a friend, the more she will see your posts in their Newsfeed.

Fill In The Blank
Have a Side Conversation

Write a message you can send a friend through Facebook Messenger if she comments on or likes one of your personal Facebook posts.

_____

_____

_____

Did You Know?
Here's George Jetson

Replying to posts and comments is the new follow up for the 21st century.

Insider Tip
The Power of Following Up

The most successful distributors in the network marketing profession believe following up with their friends until they are ready to become a customer or distributor is one of the keys to success. Facebook allows the best follow-up I have seen in my 20-year career.

My mentor and friend, Mark Yarnell, taught me that I should follow up with my friends every six months. He felt that every six months most people go through a life change that could make them open to looking at your business.

I listened to him. Every six months I called friends I hadn't spoken with in half a year. I believe this was one of the reasons I consistently enrolled 30 new distributors per month under his mentorship.

A special day in my memory illustrates the power of follow up. It was a Saturday and the last day of the month—the day that determined the company's top enroller for the year. I revisited my list and called about 600 people I spoke to six months prior. By midnight, I had enrolled 18 new distributors and became the top enroller in the company.

I've thought about the six-month follow-up many times since that accomplishment. I always wondered—what if I spoke to someone on month five of his life change? This meant that by the time I would call at the six-month mark, he might already have joined another business. This happened to me quite a few times.

Facebook creates follow-up in real-time, not in six months-time. The moment someone likes or comments on one of my posts, it gives me the opportunity to reach out to him via Messenger, which becomes the follow-up. I no longer have to call or email. People come to me.

Keep in mind that if you send a private message to your friend every time he likes or comments on a business post, you'll come across as a salesperson. They'll stop liking or commenting, and you'll lose him forever.

On the other hand, if it's been more than 90 days since you spoke to him about business, you could say, "Thanks for liking my post yesterday about how I'm enjoying sharing my products with others. How have you been? I know it's been a few months since we talked about my products. However, if you want a sample, please let me know." Then include a personal testimony so your friend can see how the product has helped you since the last time you spoke.

Do you see how I am laid back in my approach? There is no need to be aggressive. This is your friend. Also, if he had that 'life change' moment, he might ask you about your business before you send a message.

Mental Check
When To Talk Business

When someone likes or comments on your business post, how do you know if you should send her a private message? Click on her name, and you will be taken to her profile. Next, click on 'message.' A history of your private messages with her will appear. Whether you've been talking to her about personal things or not at all, if it's been more than three months since the last time you spoke to her about your network marketing business, it's okay to talk about it.

Exercise
Tally It Up

Let's make sure you know how to reply to posts and comments.

Today, go through your Facebook posts for the last seven days. Each post may have likes, comments, and shares.

How many are personal posts? _____

How many are business posts? _____

What is the total number of likes and comments for all personal and business posts over the last seven days? _____ (This number represents the amount of people you can have a one on one conversation with this week. Exciting!)

For those who liked and commented on your personal posts, send a message through Facebook Messenger thanking your friends for liking or commenting on the post. Your goal is to say hi. Don't talk about business. Only do this exercise with friends you haven't spoken to in the last 90 days. This is one way to build strong relationships with your friends.

How many friends have you done this exercise with? _____

Next, do the same exercise for your business posts. Thank your friends as well, but ask if your friends would like a sample. The 90-day rule is still in effect for these types of posts as well. This is one way to follow up with friends who are not yet customers or distributors.

How many friends have you done this exercise with? _____

By completing these exercises, you'll learn how easy it is to stay in touch (follow up) with friends by doing quality posts and interacting with those who like or comment on your quality posts. You might be surprised how many friends you lost touch with in the later exercises because you haven't communicated with them privately over the last 90 days.

Responding To Your Friend's Posts

Knowledge Check 9.7 (Circle your answer)		

T	F	By interacting with a friend, she will see you as a real friend, not someone trying to sell her products each time she talks to you.
T	F	When commenting on other people's posts, be controversial.

Fill In The Blank
Likes & Comments Make People Happy

In the last seven days, how many of your friends' posts have you commented on or liked from your Newsfeed?

_____

Your Facebook Newsfeed (what you see when you click on 'Home') is personalized to you. It's filled with your friends' posts and people you're following. They cannot see each other's posts unless they are also friends with each other.

Did You Know?
Attention Grabbing & Conversation Creation

People like posts that catch their attention and comment when they have something to say about the post.

Insider Tip
Building Relationships

Theodore Roosevelt once said, "People don't care how much you know until they know how much you care."

The easiest way I found to show people how much I care is to like and comment on their Facebook posts. It's quick, easy, and can be done in 10-20 minutes a day.

Let me share two stories.

- I became Facebook friends with Dennis. We both liked and commented on each other's posts for many months. This simple act started a conversation that led to him writing an article in a prominent Facebook blog about the success I was having helping network marketing companies on Facebook.

Insider Tip (continued)
Building Relationships

- I also became Facebook friends with Marla. Just like Dennis, Marla and I liked and commented on each other's posts. We left genuine comments because our posts interested each other and we respected our friendship. Within a short period of time, Marla, who was a writer for *Inc.* magazine, wrote an article about my contribution to helping entrepreneurs succeed on Facebook.

Both relationships started off with a genuine interest in getting to know each other by liking and commenting on each other's posts. When you care about others, they will care about you and be willing to help you.

Mental Check
Facebook Is Just Like Life

You and your family attend a local park. While enjoying the scenery, you notice a friend playing with his puppy. You smile because it's one of the cutest things you ever saw. Would you walk over to your friend and have a conversation with him about the puppy? Absolutely!

This time, you and your family don't attend a local park. You stay home because your daughter is not feeling well. While surfing through Facebook, you see an adorable picture of your friend playing with his puppy at the local park. Since you can't walk over to him and have a conversation, wouldn't you comment on his post and have a digital conversation? Definitely!

By having a digital conversation the same way you would offline, it brings you and your friends closer together than ever before.

Exercise
Engage

Let's make sure you understand how to reply to your friend's posts.

Some distributors scroll through the Newsfeed, reading friends' posts but not liking or commenting on them. Others like the posts, but hardly comment. Many comment but hardly like. Spend 20 minutes scrolling through your Newsfeed, liking and commenting on as many posts as possible.

How many posts did you like? _____

How many posts did you comment? _____

By completing this exercise, you'll interact more with your friends' posts than ever before. Better interaction means a deeper friendships. The deeper the relationships, the more likely your friends are to sample your product or consider being a distributor. Relationships happen faster when you comment more than just like.

Save Time By Using Facebook Lists

		Knowledge Check 9.8 (Circle your answer)
T	F	By liking and commenting on posts in your Prospect list, you're staying in touch with those who told you at one point they were not interested in your business.
T	F	By liking and commenting on posts in your Customer list, you're getting them to like you so you can sell a lot more product. It doesn't matter if you are friends with them.
T	F	By liking and commenting on posts in your Sample list, you're staying in touch with those who are trying or have tried your product. It gives you the opportunity to build a deeper relationship, which can lead to them telling their friends about your product and becoming a customer.
T	F	By liking and commenting on posts in your Team list, you're building deeper relationships with your distributors. This personal support allows you to not have to speak with these people on the phone or meet with them face to face.

Fill In The Blank
Lists

List the names of your Facebook friend lists and their purpose.

Friend List	Purpose
_____	_____
_____	_____
_____	_____
_____	_____
_____	_____
_____	_____

Facebook creates their own lists called Smart lists. Smart lists create themselves and automatically stay updated based on profile information you and your friends have in common (ex: work, school, family, city).

Insider Tip
Staying Organized With Lists

Throughout my career, I have always separated my friends into lists. Every person to whom I spoke about business fell into my Prospect list. If I gave a friend a sample of my product, I moved him out of the Prospect list and into my Sample list. If he became a customer or distributor, I took him out of the Sample list and put him in either a Customer or Team list. Before Facebook, I created these lists in a notebook. Lists helped me stay on top of who and how frequently to contact.

Imagine my excitement when Facebook introduced friends lists. Keeping thousands of people organized on paper was not easy.

Facebook Friends lists are much more than just being organized. The lists are social. You can interact with them in real-time to build business.

Also, I love how lists optimize your day.

Suppose you have 10 minutes to build your business because you have a family event to attend after work. How can you possibly like and comment on 300 of your friends' Facebook posts? Some days, you just run out of time. When this happens, narrow your 300 friends down to a smaller list. Click on the Prospects list and like and comment on their posts. Do you have an extra few minutes? Like and comment on Sample, Customers, and Team lists.

Using friends' lists will keep your business organized, efficient, and productive.

Mental Check
Lists = Visibility & Efficiency

By using lists effectively, you can spend 10-15 minutes a day talking to those people who matter most to your business.

Mental Check (continued)
Lists = Visibility & Efficiency

If operate inefficiently, without lists, Facebook sees you not interacting with some friends and you will stop seeing their posts in your newsfeed.

You may forget about these people since you have hundreds of friends. What if this neglected group contained people who could skyrocket your business?

Exercise
Rocking Your Lists

Let's make sure you understand how to use Facebook lists.

Spend a few minutes in each list we suggested for you, your smart lists, and other lists you created by liking and commenting on the posts.

- How many posts did you like and comment in your Prospect list? _____

- How many posts did you like and comment in your Sample list? _____

- How many posts did you like and comment in your Customer list? _____

- How many posts did you like and comment in your Team list? _____

- How many posts did you like and comment in your (   ) list? _____

- How many posts did you like and comment in your (   ) list? _____

- How many posts did you like and comment in your (   ) list? _____

- How many posts did you like and comment in your (   ) list? _____

- How many posts did you like and comment in your (   ) list? _____

Exercise (continued)

Rocking Your Lists

Uncovering hidden moments in your day will allow you to effectively use Facebook lists from your mobile phone. Consider the time you have available throughout the day by answering the following two questions. Is it possible that you could use this time to build your business? Use that time to change your future.

1. How long does it take you to stop in at your favorite coffee shop for your morning coffee? _____

2. How many television shows do you watch in which you sit through commercials? _____

By completing these exercises, you'll see the power in Facebook lists and where you can find the time throughout the day to utilize these lists. Being efficient on Facebook using lists allows you to unleash Facebook's power for your business in a short period of time.

Final Thoughts

It's important to know how to balance your personal and business life through your Facebook posts, how to use the 80/20 rule, how to share and add company posts, how often should you post, how to professionally reply to posts and comments and respond to your friend's posts, and how to optimize your time by using Facebook lists so you are not on Facebook for hours a day.

Remember, people become customers and distributors with friends, not strangers. Have fun on Facebook by making friendships stronger with your Facebook friends. It will lead to good business.

What are your five biggest takeaways from this chapter?

1. _____

2. _____

3. _____

4. _____

5. _____

NOTES:

Chapter 10

Grow Your Friends To Grow Your Income

W hat would you do if more than one billion people were standing outside your home waiting to hear about your business right now?

Besides running around the house jumping for joy, you'd have an endless supply of potential customers and distributors, as long as you're willing to take the time to build a relationship with each person.

Let's learn how Graph Search on Facebook grows your business.

Take a few minutes now to reread or skim chapter 11 in *Network Marketing For Facebook* before completing this workbook section.

		Knowledge Check 10.1 (Circle your answer)
T	F	Without much effort, Graph Search allows you to connect with people from your past.
T	F	To use Graph Search, type phrases into the Facebook search box.
T	F	By changing one word in Graph Search you will be given a fresh list of possible new friends.
T	F	As you search for new Facebook friends, you'll come across people you already know. It's best to add them to an Interest list.
T	F	When reconnecting with old friends, it's okay to talk about your business immediately.
T	F	Add as many friends as you like per day when using Graph Search.

As you search for new Facebook friends, you'll come across people you already know. It's best to do which of the following?

a. Add them as a friend, but don't send a private message since you already know them.
b. Send a private message and wait for them to reply before you send a friend request.
c. Add them as a friend and send a private message.
d. None of the above
e. All of the above

As you search for new Facebook friends, you'll come across people you don't yet know but wish to befriend. It's best to do which of the following?

a. Add them as a friend and send a private message.
b. Add them to an interest list.
c. Send a private message and wait for them to reply before you send a friend request.
d. All of the above
e. None of the above.

Fill In The Blank
Write It Down

Do you currently use Graph Search? Why or why not?

_____

_____

Did You Know?
Knowledge Check

1.5 billion searches happen daily on Facebook.

Insider Tip
Using Graph Search

Here are how two people, Chris and Brian, played a role in my business because of Graph Search and a few thoughts.

Chris:	A few years ago, I used Graph Search to reconnect with friends from high school. –Chris was one such person. We weren't close friends in high school, but I remembered him. A couple of months after we became Facebook friends, he sent a message that went something like this … "Hey, Jim! I see you're always talking about business and how to make money. My wife and I are looking at ways to make extra money. Since we went to high school together, I trust you. Can you give me some advice?"
Brian:	When someone impresses me because I read his book or see her in a magazine, I use Graph Search to find him or her on Facebook. I found Brian from a magazine I read. In my eyes, he was a Facebook Advertising God. I used an Interest list to follow Brian on Facebook. After a while, Brian liked one of my comments on his post. I sent him a friend request. Brian and I have been friends ever since. Brian has since confirmed with me that he is a Facebook Advertising God. Also a Comedy God. Also a Workbook Editing God who puts words in my mouth. When connecting with new friends who might not know you, using an Interest list is almost always the right next step. An Interest list allows you to follow your new friend, liking and commenting on his posts before you send a friend request. It gives your new friend an opportunity to know, like, and trust you. Once this new friend interacts with your comments, send him a friend request. Once he accepts your friend request, he'll start to see your posts, both personal and business.

You might be wondering if any business came of my relationship with Brian. His full name is Brian Carter.

Here are a few more thoughts I have about Graph Search.

Thought:	Graph Search can be overwhelming, even to the most advanced Facebook user.
	For the network marketing professional, try this fun and easy basic search: people who live in (city, state). Now you have access to every person in that city who has a Facebook account, as long as they filled in their 'current city' on their profile.
	Another fun search: Females who live in (city, state). Now you narrowed the search down to only females.
	The results of these two searches, alone, could keep you busy for the rest of your network marketing career, and you still haven't searched for people who went to your high school or college, or past co-workers.
Thought:	Adding new Facebook friends is exciting. The excitement will only last if most of these friends accept your friend request. Keep the following in mind. Before someone accepts your friend request, they'll visit your profile to read your work history, where you went to school, where you live, where you have lived, your hometown, and more.
	Most people on Facebook are as open to a friend request as they are to a friendship in real life. They must believe a real friendship with you could happen. That belief comes from seeing mutual friends and commonalities in your profile.
Thought:	As your new friends are accepting your friend requests, be respectful of your new relationship. Cherish it because it can be gone tomorrow. If you focus on becoming real friends with these new people, I promise something wonderful will come out of each new relationship for your business. It might take three days or three years, but it will happen.

Thought:	I share the following with distributors I coach one on one.

- Every day, send 10 new people a friend request with a meaningful and heartfelt message ONLY if you know these people or have a strong connection. For example, your best friend is a mutual friend or you both went to the same high school.

- Once 10 new people become easy, increase the number to 20. Never friend request more than 30 per day. Once you go beyond 10, always make sure you never do more than 10 within a four-hour time frame.

- Repeat the same numbers above with people you don't know, but put these people in an Interest list instead of sending a friend request.

- If you are full-time in the network marketing profession, I encourage you to contact 60 people a day using the following formula:

- 20 in the morning (10 friend requests, 10 Interest list)

- 20 in the afternoon (10 friend requests, 10 Interest list)

- 20 in the evening (10 friend requests, 10 Interest list)

- If you do 60 requests per day, this equates to 1,800 new people a month who might become a customer or distributor.

These numbers will only be successful if you take time to build a relationship with these people. Distributors who focus on business only will fail miserably, and Facebook might even block you from doing any type of activity on the site for a long time. If you are in the network marketing profession to create a lifelong income for you and your family, look forward to using Graph Search to help you achieve success.

You may feel overwhelmed, still not understanding how big Graph Search is for your business. You may find it awkward to reach out to people through Graph Search. Consider the following.

Overwhelmed:	Keep it fun and simple. You can find more than enough people through Graph Search right in your own back yard, even though there seemingly unlimited ways to connect with people all around the world.
Still don't understand:	• Let's say you reach out to 10 new people a day. This should take about 15 minutes. Every month, that adds up to about 280 new potential customers or distributors. • After one year, your Facebook Prospect list has grown to 3,360. • What if you already have 10 distributors on your team, and they do the same thing? Then, within a year, your Facebook Prospect list has grown to 40,320. Where else can you create a list of 40,320 people who know, like, and trust you and 10 of your distributors in 12 months?
Awkward:	One way to make it less awkward to reach out to someone you don't yet know is by using the right words. Here's an example of how easy it is to chat with people on Facebook: Hey, Sara! It's nice to meet you! I'm also from (your city). The reason I reached out to you is because I'm looking to make new friends in my area. I noticed we have 10 mutual friends and one of them is Alexa Bistall. How long have you been friends? I went to high school with Alexa. Looking forward to connecting. I've lived in the area for 13 years. I'm a stay-at-home mom with two little girls, and I work from home. Love to hear from you.

Exercise
A Ton of Potential Customers

Let's make sure you understand how to use Graph Search for your business.

Type the following phrases into Facebook's Graph Search. Next to each phrase, write how many people Facebook introduced to you. Get ready to be excited!

- Friends of my friends: _____

- People from (enter your hometown): _____

- People who live in (insert a town/state): _____

- People who graduated from (insert your high school) in (insert your graduation year): _____

- People who graduated from (insert your college) in (insert your graduation year): _____

- People who work at (name of your current or past employer): _____

- People who like (enter your favorite hobby): _____

- Pages liked by people who are my age: _____

Next, come up with your own phrases to find people. Write the phrases below.

_____

_____

_____

_____

_____

_____

By completing these exercises, you'll learn about Facebook's ability to connect you with infinite business prospects. Never running out of people with whom to speak eliminates one of the top reasons why you and your distributors could fail in the network marketing profession.

Final Thoughts

The biggest reason distributors fail is they don't have a constant stream of new connections. Graph Search solves this problem by opening

Facebook's entire database to you. All you need to do is take the time to reach out and build relationships with the more than one billion people Facebook users around the world.

What are your five biggest takeaways from this chapter?

1. _____

2. _____

3. _____

4. _____

5. _____

NOTES:

Chapter 11

How Birthday Wishes Create Business Success

How would you feel if, every year, more than 100 people joined together to sing "Happy Birthday" to you? Besides feeling fantastic and connected to others, you'd also have an opportunity to talk about your business to those you care about most.

Let's learn how Happy Birthdays on Facebook grow your business.

Take a few minutes now to reread or skim chapter 12 in *Network Marketing For Facebook* before completing this workbook section.

		Knowledge Check 11.1 (Circle your answer)
T	F	Wishing someone a happy birthday on Facebook is one simple act that builds a stronger relationship.
T	F	Never talk about your products if a conversation starts after wishing someone a happy birthday, even if an opportunity arises.
T	F	Wishing a Facebook friend a happy birthday can allow you to reconnect with someone to whom you haven't spoken in a while.
T	F	The following is an effective example of how to wish someone a happy birthday while network marketing on Facebook. *Happy Birthday, Mark! How does it feel to hit the big 5-0?*
T	F	The following is an effective example of how to wish someone a happy birthday while network marketing on Facebook. *Happy Birthday, Alicia! What are you doing for fun to celebrate your special day? Also, I just got started in my own business. Can I send you a sample of my product?*

Knowledge Check 11.1 (continued)
(Circle your answer)

T	F	The following is an effective example of how to wish someone a happy birthday while network marketing on Facebook.

Happy Birthday, Jeremy! I saw the picture of you and your son at his basketball game a couple of weeks ago. You guys looked like you were having so much fun. Do you travel much? I have a great travel discount program if you want to take a look. It would make for a nice birthday present.

Fill In The Blank
People Love When You Wish Them Happy Birthday

Do you currently wish your friends a happy birthday on Facebook? Why or why not?

_____

_____

_____

Did You Know?
This Is Why We're Old

Everyone has a birthday on Facebook every year

Insider Tip
Birthday Messages in Action

Here is a sample message, past experience, and a few thoughts that might help you with the idea of happy birthdays on Facebook.

Sample Message:	Wishing someone a happy birthday through Messenger might lead your friend to ask, "What have you been up to?" This question gives you the opportunity to talk about your business.

Sample Message:	A nice response might be: "I'm still working at Sol's Accounting, and it's going well. Tom and the baby are doing wonderful. We're thinking about having a second child, so we got creative and started a fun home-based business to offset the additional expenses. My friend is promoting a skincare business, so Tom and I sampled the product. It did wonders for my dry skin. It made sense to share it with others and earn extra money. I'd love to send you a sample. It's not just for dry skin. If you use lotion or wash your face you will want to try it out ☺ … More importantly, Sarah, I just wanted to reach out and say happy birthday. I hope your day is going awesome!"
Past Experience:	Here is an example from my own life while living in Scottsdale, Arizona. After reading, *The Social Media Bible* by Lon Safko, I friended him on Facebook. *The Social Media Bible* is one of the most successful social media books of all time. Soon after, it was his birthday. Here is how it went: Jim: *Happy Birthday!* Lon: *Thank You! We need to connect soon!* The outcome? I sent him my phone number, and we chatted on the phone. He came to my office, and I helped him create his own Facebook Business Page and strategy. I had no intentions on doing business with him. I only wanted to wish him a happy birthday.
Thoughts:	When I wish my friends a happy birthday, it comes from the heart. I am genuine, and I really mean it. I'm not thinking about business, even though business might come from it. Sometimes you can give one of your products, a full-size and not a sample, as a gift during the happy birthday wishes. I recommend doing this only for someone you consider a real friend, someone for whom you would buy a present outside of Facebook.

Insider Tip (continued)
Birthday Messages in Action

Thoughts:	For example you might say, "Happy Birthday, Karen! I bet you're having a wonderful day. I love seeing your pictures on Facebook, especially the one yesterday of your precious little girl. May I have your address? I have something small and special I would like to send to you."
	The biggest takeaway is that it's better to wish someone a happy birthday through Messenger than the wall because it creates a one-on-one conversation. That conversation stands out more to your friend than the hundreds of greetings she may receive on her profile timeline. She is more likely to see it. The greeting is also more likely to be personal.

Mental Check
An Excuse To Say Hi

Wishing someone a happy birthday is a first great step to building a long lasting relationship. You can say, "Hello, Mark! I know we haven't spoken on Facebook, yet we are Facebook friends. I just wanted to wish you a happy birthday!"

Exercise
Start Wishing

Let's make sure you understand how birthday wishes create business success.

Every day, wake up in the morning and check birthday notifications on Facebook. List three Facebook friends who celebrate birthdays this week.

1. _____

2. _____

3. _____

Next, go to each of these three Facebook friends' profiles and learn something about each one of them. Send each friend a private message, wishing a happy birthday. Make your message meaningful by talking about what you learned on your friend's profile. Build a relationship. Using the lines below, write one thing you learned from each friend's profile.

Friend (1) _____
_____

Friend (2) _____
_____

Friend (3) _____
_____

Now, combine what you learned with a genuine happy birthday using the lines below. Use this message on Facebook.

Friend (1) _____
_____

Friend (2) _____
_____

Friend (3) _____
_____

By completing these exercises, you'll wish your friend a happy birthday with a more meaningful message. These messages will touch the heart of your friends and create a better relationship. And sometimes, these messages will allow you to talk about business.

What Should You Do When Someone Wishes You A Happy Birthday

T	F	Each birthday wish is not an open invitation to talk about your products.

Knowledge Check 11.2 (continued)
(Circle your answer)

T	F	We suggest sending each person a thank you message through the private message feature.
T	F	The following is an effective example of how to respond. *Thank you for the birthday wishes! I have an opportunity I would love to share with you. You probably hate your job like the rest of my friends. Would you be interested in making an extra $10,000 a month?*
T	F	The following is an effective example of how to respond. *Thank you for the birthday wishes! Being healthy has become a #1 priority for my family. We even started a business around it. We helped a few friends lose weight and earn some extra money. We were blessed this year!*
T	F	The following is an effective example of how to respond. *Thank you for the birthday wishes! This past year has been wonderful for my family. We are making over a $100,000 a year working from home and hardly working to earn it. You can, too. Do you want to check it out?*
T	F	The following is an effective example of how to respond. *Thank you for the birthday wishes! This past year has been insane! We no longer pay for our electricity bill and we're also getting paid off of everyone in town as well. I feel like I won the lottery. We're blessed and you should be, too! Do you want more info?*
T	F	The following is an effective example of how to respond. *Thank you for the birthday wishes! This past year we found a product to help our son's eczema. It worked so well on our son that we decided to share it with others for some extra money. It's been a fun year!*
T	F	The following is an effective example of how to respond *Thank you for the birthday wishes! We've been traveling for free all year because of our home-based business. Would you like to travel for free as well? It's unreal.*

Fill In The Blank
Another Excuse To Interact

Do you currently respond to everyone who wishes you a happy birthday? Why or why not?

_____

_____

Did You Know?
Focus on Relationships

Your Facebook friends can tell when you respond back to build a real friendship or to make money with your network marketing business. The stats on spam email confirm that prospects judge very quickly whether your online messaging is personal or fake. 69% of email recipients report email as Spam based solely on the subject line, and 35% of email recipients open email based on the subject line alone. People can tell your motive within a few words. Stay focused on building a real relationship.

Insider Tip
Birthdays Create Business

Here is an example of how thanking someone who wished you a happy birthday could turn into business.

Alexa wishes you a happy birthday on your wall. You send her a private message.

You: "Hey, Alexa! Thanks for the birthday wishes! How have you been?"

Alexa: "I'm doing great! Thanks for asking. Planning a vacation at the moment. Trying to decide on St. Thomas or Bahamas. Any suggestions?"

You: "Definitely St. Thomas! Richard and I went there for our 10th anniversary. Absolutely stunning! By the way, I been meaning to ask you … over the last six months, I've lost 22 pounds and 14 inches. Would you have an interest in checking out the product I am using? Because of my results, I started sharing it with friends and family to earn some extra money."

Alexa: "Sure, I would love to learn more."

You never know what opportunities will arise just from saying thank you.

Mental Check
Deepen a Friendship

Responding to happy birthday wishes is an opportunity to get to know someone better. Since that person reached out to you, she will most likely welcome a response. You can say, "Hello, Theresa! I know we haven't spoken on Facebook, but I want to thank you for wishing me a happy birthday. Please tell me more about yourself."

Let's make sure you understand what to do when someone wishes you a happy birthday.

Review your last birthday on Facebook to get an understanding of how you currently handle birthday wishes.

How many Facebook friends wished you a happy birthday?

_____

Out of those who wished you a happy birthday, how many did you thank for the well-wishes? _____

Who are three friends to whom you did not respond?

1. _____

2. _____

3. _____

Next, send each of these friends a thank you message through private message. If your birthday was more than a few months old, you can say, "Hey! I apologize for the epic delay. I just wanted to say thank you for wishing me a happy birthday. How is life treating you?" Using the lines below, write your friends' responses.

Friend (1) _____

_____

Friend (2) _____

_____

Friend (3) _____

_____

By completing these exercises, you'll see how powerful it is to respond to those who wish you a happy birthday. Appreciation goes a long way in this world, so recognize people for their kind gestures.

Final Thoughts

Do you believe wishing someone a happy birthday creates business success?

It's the simple things in life, like wishing someone a happy birthday, that lead to more customers, distributors, and referrals.

What are your five biggest takeaways from this chapter?

1. _____

2. _____

3. _____

4. _____

5. _____

NOTES:

Conclusion

We want you to be successful, and we're excited to hear how our workbook has helped you! Please visit us at www.facebook.com/networkmarketingforsocialmedia to share your successes. Thank you for allowing us to be part of your journey.

Answer Key

Chapter 1
1.1: T, T
1.2: F, b
1.3: T, T, a, d
1.4: T, F, T, f
1.5: T, d
1.6: F, T
1.7: F, F, T, e
1.8: T
1.9: T, d
1.10: T, e

Chapter 2
2.1: F, F, c
2.2: f, f, f, f, f, b, f, d, f

Chapter 3
3.1: T, e
3.2: T, F
3.3: T, F, a, e
3.4: F
3.5: T, F, F, c
3.6: F, T, T, T, e, b
3.7: F, F

Chapter 4
4.1: T, F, T
4.2: F, T, a, e
4.3: F, T, F, e, e
4.4: F, T, e
4.5: T
4.6: T
4.7: F
4.8: F
4.9: T
4.10: T

Chapter 5
5.1: c
5.2: F, F, T, F, T, F, T
5.3: T, F

Chapter 6
6.1: T, F, T
6.2: F, T
6.3: T, F, F, T, F, F, T
6.4: F, T
6.5: F, F, T, T

Chapter 7
7.1: T, F, T, F
7.2: F, F, T
7.3: F, T, F, T
7.4: T, T, F
7.5: F, T, F, F
7.6: T, T, F, F

Chapter 8
8.1: F, T

Chapter 9
9.1: F, T, T
9.2: T, F, F, T, T, T
9.3: F, F
9.4: F, T, T, F, F, T, T
9.5: T, F, F, T
9.6: F, F, T
9.7: T, F
9.8: T, F, T, F

Chapter 10
10.1: T, T, T, F, F, F, c, b

Chapter 11
11.1: T, F, T, T, F, F
11.2: F, T, F, T, F, F, T, F

Reviews of The Book

"Jim Lupkin and Brian know their stuff with social media. Buy the book. I bought the book. It's awesome." - Kevin Thompson

"This book is a must for those wanting to build a strong team online. With all the books out there claiming to help grow your presence on Facebook this is a tool that actually works. From this book I have realized I have spent too much of my time posting to a very small audience on my Facebook fan page and no time on what my team actually see's which is the group page posts. This is a must read and it will give you a strategy on how to build your team online." - Royce-Willis

"I'm thankful for all that you have taught me and how I've watched you help others and companies grow as well is very commendable!, Great training, easy to follow and understand!" - Debbie Bales

"This was an easy and informative read! I learned so much from this book and I really love the practical, simple terms and down to earth teachings from Jim and Brian. I feel like anyone can use the principles and techniques and apply them and find success through Facebook and other social media. I have been doing quite a few things wrong and I look forward to correcting my ways and moving forward with my eyes opened to new possibilities. I highly recommend this book and know anyone can gain valuable information to help you find success in your business!" - Stephanie Macula

"I just finished reading this book and have highly encouraged everyone on my team to purchase it and apply the outstanding tips and lessons found within it. While initially skeptical on how to incorporate a network marketing business into Facebook, Jim's tips provide a way to use the platform most effectively and without alienating friends. I have already seen direct and positive results by following his step by step instruction! Order it, read it and most importantly…TAKE ACTION on his tips to grow your business through Facebook! It will only complement and accelerate success of whatever you are already doing! Congratulations on a great book Jim and Brian!" - Todd Anderson

"I read Network Marketing for Facebook in one day and gained so much knowledge. Great information and interviews. What I liked the best was that 2 scenarios were given; good vs. the bad way of doing things. Also there was examples on how to open, engage and follow up in a conversation. In addition I liked learning about Jim Lupkin and his wife, they know and have been in network marketing, product of the product. Thank you again." - LaFabiola Hurtado

"AMAZING BOOK!! Thanks for giving us REAL advise that WORKS! I have several team members loving it too! We are using this to take it to the next level! Thanks for helping us become professionals!" - Karen Aycock

"I highly recommend this book to all Network Marketing Professionals. Jim and Brian do a good job of showing the importance of using Facebook in you networking strategy in a clear and understandable way. I look forward to reading anything these authors release!! I have started using some of the simple strategies from the book and been able to increase my engagement on my Facebook page." - Dennis Taylor

"I am currently only half way through the book but wanted to write a review and share the excellent results I have gotten already. Just by implementing a few of his tips on Facebook marketing I have increased my contacts on Facebook by over 60 in one week. Highly recommend to anyone looking for advice on social media marketing." - Talitha Adkins

"This is a MUST-DOWNLOAD for anyone in the Network Marketing field looking to be successful on Facebook. You don't have to create a separate account or let your network marketing business take over your newsfeed and spam your friends to grow your business. You can still be yourself and use the strategies and tactics within this book to make authentic and long-lasting business relationships with your connections. This book gives you the exact steps to use when it comes to introducing your friends to your product on Facebook. Social media does not have to be complicated. This book by Jim and Brian makes it easy!" - Christina Brown

"This book is exactly what every Network Marketer needs. Social Media is a huge part of today's society and if you are not utilizing it to your advantage then you are definitely missing out. Not only on sales but on building quality relationships. As a friend of Jim's I know he has the knowledge and experience to back up his claims. I've personally been mentored by him and have seen firsthand how the content in this book works." - James Maldonado

"Incredible content of the etiquette in using Facebook to build your business. Simple steps that really are exactly how any business is built, thru developing relationships, finding out what they need, and then offering them a way to solve their need. Was inspiring to read the testimonials from true leaders in our industry that used Facebook in several different ways to rapidly build a global network marketing business. Jim shares step by step how to engage personally with your Facebook audience to attract them to you properly. Thank you Jim for giving this information to encourage us to utilize social media to our advantage but to not forget the basics." - Wendy Abner

"I just finished reading the book on Kindle and went back and bought the paperback edition so I could keep it on my bookshelf as a ready reference book. Jim and Brian have created a must have tool for everyone in network marketing who want to harness the power of Facebook to better build their business. This book is filled with solid, proven advice and very useable guidelines on how to better build your business using Facebook. Every distributor in my organization will be encouraged to pick up a copy and have their team do the same." - Larry Louzon

"This is an amazing book! It is designed for primarily the passion driven networker but can also be used by any professional who truly wants to "expand their territory" and hasn't truly understood how to utilize FB in balanced way! I have spent hundreds of dollars on videos and courses to help build a great FB audience and have some success However, this book has step by step principals to truly build relationships using social media as an intro. along with avoiding some of the pitfalls. I loved the testimonials of all the people who have had different levels of success applying the principals shared in this book. Thank you Jim for taking the time to share your wisdom with the world and I am looking forward to working together!" - Andrea London

"This is a great book for every person in network marketing. It shows step by step how to successfully post and build relationships on Facebook. I highly recommend this book." - Ann Stone

"Here is something major you are going to love about this book: it's very practical, not just theoretical. Jim & Brian get you on the fast-track to success using Facebook for your business. Their truth is simple – and it really works! I used to think sites like Facebook were a waste of time, but after starting my network marketing business, I knew I'd be foolish not learning how to properly use social media. Since then, I've been successfully converting new business from a global list of prospects, using Facebook at the core of my social media strategy. I encourage you to take a deep breath, step out of your comfort zone, and just follow what you are taught in this book. Do it today; you'll be glad you did by tomorrow." - Monique O'Reilly

"Just read through Network Marketing for Facebook and I have to say that this book is the definitive book on how to use Facebook to build a business through building relationships. I have chased my tail trying to figure out how to capitalize on the huge marketplace that Facebook is, and for the first time, Network Marketing for Facebook has laid out a clear, and simple, step by step approach to developing a plan, and implementing it. The authors, and the impressive testimonials, make it very clear that marketing online is no different than marketing offline – gotta build those relationships and develop a level of trust. I highly recommend this book to anyone looking to grow their business the correct way using social media." - Michael Hayes

"I finished the first half of this book and have already learned so I much! I also learned that I've already made several mistakes, but that I can turn those into successes quite easily!! This is a must read if you want to be successful in building your business." - Alexanne Bennett

"I just finished reading "Network Marketing for Facebook" for the 1st time. I say for the 1st time, because I know it is a book I will re-read and refer to over and over again. I just heard about the book on a team conference call last night, I immediately bought it and downloaded it, and I have not been able to put it down! It has so many tips and tricks and strategies that any entrepreneur can apply immediately, not just for a Network Marketing company, but for any kind of business, really. The book is in 2 parts. The first half of the book is real-life tips, strategies and scripts that you can start to implement right away to help build your venture. It shows the right way to use Facebook and other social media to properly expose your business and to generate interest, instead of just blatantly and endlessly promoting the business, which is what many people do. The second half of the book is profiles and interviews with Network Marketing professionals who have benefited from author Jim Lupkin's advice, friendship, and guidance over the years. They share their struggles and successes with the industry and social media, and they all give you very helpful and valuable nuggets to help you build a business. I think this book is a must read for any home-based business entrepreneur, and especially for those who want to build a successful, long-term business using Facebook and social media as a tool to do so. I would highly and wholeheartedly recommend this book to anybody in the Network Marketing profession, whether it be the seasoned pro, or the newbie, and everybody in between. I look forward to using the strategies that are described in this book to build my own business, to share my products and to help my team do the same. Thank you for a great guide, Jim!" - Tom Fragale

"Every network marketer needs to read this book! Jim and Brian give practical, doable steps on how to market yourself and business on Facebook. After reading this book, I realized that I was not using social media correctly or consistently enough to grow a successful business. I messaged Jim on FB with some questions, he responded quickly and told me to follow his training and get prepared to be successful. Well, that's exactly what I'm going to do, he provided the roadmap and I'm going to follow it!" - Rhoda Murray

"Normally, I read straight through a book; however, in this one, I have been taking the time to digest all the ideas, so I recommend highlighting, taking notes, and rereading key concepts in small chunks to allow time to digest all the information and effectively put it into practice. Strategic thinking is the key to success, and this book offers great doable strategies to boost any business." - Nancy Guss

"Network Marketing/MLM is a form of distribution many companies choose to use today to move their product, from the factory to the end consumer, through independent reps/consumers. This form of distribution is proving to be one of the most effective ways for selling new technologies and products that need to be touched and shared by knowledgeable users/consumers/reps. My original MLM mentors, in the early 1990s, were Art Napolitano and Jeff Olson who happen to be legends in this industry. I do believe Jim Lupkin possesses many of the great qualities of these proven leaders and knowledge they don't have. In this book, Jim shares how to use one of the greatest marketing tools direct sales professionals have ever had an opportunity to use to market the products and the opportunity they love. What is the tool? Facebook. I highly recommend you purchase this book, if you are serious about building a profitable MLM distribution business. Thanks Jim and Brian for sharing your knowledge." - Mark Johnson

"I love the book. The book is easy to read it simply explains Network marketing for Facebook. It covers Profile Pics, cover photos, groups and more. I love the examples of everyday people and how they learned what to do. I can relate to the examples. I will be finishing the book soon and keeping the book ready to review frequently. I plan on buying more hard cover copies of the book. I highly recommend for anyone and everyone to BUY THE BOOK !!!!" - Matthew Babiak

"Great book! It was an easy read and easy to understand techniques. If you're looking to expand your business using Facebook you will love it!" - Aime Davis

"Love It! Detailed and to the point about how to Market successfully on Fb. I do believe I will purchase this for my downline. Great tool for sure. This book is a Must Have!" - Jana McKey

"I've been in direct sales for more than 8 years and I'm always looking to learn more about growing my business. This book hit the nail on the head in terms of growing with Facebook (and can be applied to other social media networks). It provided easy to follow steps and suggestions, along with scripts to follow to create conversation and ultimately grow your business. I especially loved at the end of the book where a few network marketing professionals that have been quite successful offered words of advice. It's always nice to hear insight from top names in MLM. Thanks for sharing your wisdom and strategy in this book!" - Catharine Small

"I have known Jim for many years, he is an expert in social media, and has a genuine love to help people succeed!" - Darren Hottinger

"This is a must have book for anyone in the Network Marketing business! A huge part of the business is building your team with a proven duplicable system. In the book there are many testimonials from people that have built huge teams using Facebook and the systems that are taught in the wonder book!" - Steve Lofton

"I absolutely LOVED this book. Although I had never personally met Jim, I knew he had a vast knowledge in this area, so couldn't wait to get his book. I already had some knowledge as I have two online businesses with Facebook Pages, and I have a network marketing business as well. Many say you can't build your network marketing business via Facebook and I wanted to prove them wrong. Now I know how to go about it. I have also had a lot more activity on my business pages since reading the book. It gave me a much better understanding on how to get people interacting on your page, and the difference has been outstanding! I believe the information about groups will be very powerful for me. The information in this book can be adjusted for traditional business as well, not just Network Marketing. So I urge anyone who is contemplating buying this book, to do it NOW. The price is incredible... I was shocked when I saw how inexpensive it was! Thanks Jim & Brian for taking the time to share your knowledge... Greatly appreciated!" - Vicki Leishman

"I have known Jim since I was a little girl. We lived on the same street growing up. I always knew he was going to do great things. His new book is AMAZING! It is for those who are seasoned network marketers, or those who are just starting out like myself. I have learned great things from this book. I look forward to using all the information in this book to be successful. This book will be a tool that I will use for a long time to come." - Kristi L. Harrington

"This book has been great for my business. It has opened up new opportunities on sharing my network marketing business! I have already shared with numerous friends who have struggled as I have with expanding my reach of potential customers and business partners!" - Lisa Crawford

"I've worked with Jim personally this past year and I know that you'll find this read invaluable. He has over 20 years of experience in the Direct Selling Industry and his insight will inspire you in ways you never thought of. Fantastic read, highly recommend!" - Lindsey Barber

"Jim, I'm more than half way through your new book and I love it! About 90 percent of my business comes from FB. I've only been on FB for two years...I started when I began sharing my product. About a month later, I had the good fortune of meeting you and hearing you at the National Conference. Your knowledge and experience have helped me so much. I have been developing relationships on FB and the ideas in your new book will help me do that even better. I'm going to 'work' through the book and make your ideas my habits. The interview section is fantastic! Not only great testimonies, but even more suggestions on how to nurture relationships using FB. The book is well written. It's easy to read and implement. I know I'll be referring to it over and over. And, I'll be recommending it to my team and others in network marketing. Thank you, Jim!!" - Linda A. Weir

"I have finished your book up to the point of the testimonials. Have read a couple of them, will try to finish it up tomorrow. For the most part, I have already done what you recommended in your book, BUT what I like best is the information you give about connecting with "long lost friends" through doing the search for things such as "people who graduated from..." "People who have the same interests..." "People who are friends with..." Thank you so much for your book and guidance. I like what you said about just connecting and taking interest in those long lost friends. I moved away from my home town and definitely don't have friends now that I went to school with. I will work on it! Thanks again!" - Keri Hall

"This easy to understand book provides ALL the information you need to begin reaching potential customers and distributors into a vastness of the market that when applied equals Helping thousands of people change their lives in unimaginable ways while providing assured success in your business." - Brenda Booker

"There is so much great advice for network marketing professionals in this book. Jim definitely made me more aware of what I am posting and how to sell without selling. My biggest issue using social media to build my business has always been how reach out and respond to people I haven't spoken to in a while. and this book takes all of the guess work out of reaching out to prospects. I very much enjoy how the book is written. Having examples of posts for each category of Network marketing company is brilliant , and makes makes the book more relatable for everyone." - Tara Chernicky

"I have to say Jim Lupkin is one of a kind . . . after reading my review on Amazon I was contacted and informed that he was updating the book based on customer feedback to remove the personal information from the interviews in the book. Wow! Authors really do listen! Since the book has been revised I feel very comfortable recommending this book, in fact it is a must read for anyone serious about building a Network Marketing business on Facebook today. I have updated my review from four stars to five because it is that good!" - Taylor Clouse